KEY WORDS of the KINGDOM

God's Words of the Kingdom for Kids!

KIM LYON

WESTBOW
PRESS®
A DIVISION OF THOMAS NELSON
& ZONDERVAN

WestBow Press books may be ordered through booksellers or by contacting:

WestBow Press
A Division of Thomas Nelson & Zondervan
1663 Liberty Drive
Bloomington, IN 47403
www.westbowpress.com
1 (866) 928-1240

ISBN: 978-1-5127-1498-2 (sc)

Library of Congress Control Number: 2015916555

Print information available on the last page.

WestBow Press rev. date: 11/10/2015

Dedication:

Your love amazes me. Dedicated back to my Father God, who has given His all, as my creator, provider, healer, teacher and friend.

Your learning amazes me. Dedicated to my grandson, whom I've learned so much from, since his birth three and a half years ago.

Your patience amazes me. Dedicated to my husband who claims I've invested 22,000 hours in writing this book.

A Special Thank You:

To Shay Meckenstock for being a very dear friend, teacher and mentor.

To the Kingdom Kids in the photos for being so agreeable and photogenic.

Shane, Ruby, Eli, Cali, Jillyan, Grace, Hope, Joy, Joseph, Joshua, Jadon, Jonah, Justin and Avery

To the adults in the photos for allowing me to choose their photos while featuring one of the Kingdom Kids. Kaley, Jerome, Michaela, Jeremy, Alice, Leroy, and Kenton

To my daughter Kaley for her photographs and proofreading, and sister Karmin for photographs.

The Kids of the Kingdom books are designed to be helpful as guidance for parents, instruction for children, and for developing an understanding of how God's Kingdom should look in the lives of families today.

Grandma, bring the Bible out of the box!

Table of Contents

God's Words of the Kingdom for Kids!   <u>**Share,Give**</u>

Lesson 1

Opening Prayer: Dear Father, please be with us today as we learn about <u>sharing</u>, as You want it to be in your Kingdom.

Scripture: Proverbs 22:9, *Generous people will be blessed, because they <u>share</u> their food with the poor.*

Vocabulary: <u>share (give)</u>

Songs: <u>The B I B L E</u>, The Wonder Kids, *30 Bible Songs and 30 Bible Stories*

<u>Jesus Loves Me,</u> The Wonder Kids, *30 Bible Songs and 30 Bible Stories*

<u>The More We Get Together</u>, Cedarmont Kids, *100 Singalong Songs for Kids*

Snack: Sharing Snack: give each child a small item to share for snack, chocolate milk

Story: <u>It's Fun to Share,</u> Ruby came to Shane's house. Shane was playing trains. He loves trains. Ruby wanted to play with Shane. Ruby wanted to play trains. The first thing Ruby did was to pick out a train to play with. It was Shane's favorite train! Shane was unhappy that Ruby wanted to play with his favorite train. He grabbed it away from Ruby. Ruby cried. Shane's mommie came in to help the kids learn to <u>share</u>. She told Shane it was a lot of fun to have Ruby play trains too. Shane got to pick out a train, and Ruby got to pick out a train. Both kids got to play with the train they chose, on the same track. All of a sudden Ruby's train was chasing Shane's train! Shane giggled and giggled. He understood it was more fun to play with a friend. He understood that he had to <u>share</u> his trains with his friend. God has so much power that He created the entire Earth and everything in it! He created it to <u>share</u> with his people. We are His people. He <u>shares</u> with us. We must learn to <u>share</u> with others.

Fine Motor: Show How to <u>Share:</u> <u>share</u> magazines and newspaper photos showing how or what people <u>share</u>

Large Motor: The <u>Sharing</u> Ball: one big ball to <u>share</u>

Activity: The <u>Sharing</u> Job: small blocks, build towers by working together

Close in Prayer: Thank You Father for <u>sharing</u> your life with us! Thank You for <u>sharing</u> your Son, Jesus with us. Help us learn to <u>share</u>. Amen

Guidance for Parents: **Share**

Scripture: Proverbs 22:9, *Generous people will be blessed, because they* <u>*share*</u> *their food with the poor.*

Ways to <u>Share</u>: The word <u>share</u> actually means 'give'. If your child is asked to <u>share</u>, it feels to the child as though he has to give the other child what he currently has or whatever is being asked of him! Giving up something that a child is choosing right at the moment is tough. This is why it takes parental guidance to teach children to share. Take turns: Talk to both children. "Shane is playing with it now. You can play with it in 2 minutes." Take enough to share: If your child is playing with trains, have an extra in your bag for your child to share. Prepare your child that this train is for sharing with others. Teachable Moment: It's o.k. to tell the other child that this toy belongs to Shane, and he's playing with it right now. It's o.k. but it's not taking advantage of an opportunity to teach your child to share. Reassure: Always reassure the child who shares that it still belongs to him/her even if another child plays with it for a while.

Songs used today:

<u>The B I B L E</u>, The Wonder Kids, *30 Bible Songs and 30 Bible Stories*
<u>Jesus Loves Me,</u> The Wonder Kids, *30 Bible Songs and 30 Bible Stories*
<u>The More We Get Together</u>, Cedarmont Kids, *100 Singalong Songs for Kids*

Vocabulary Builder: <u>share, give</u>

Teaching Tidbit: Learning to <u>share</u> is a developmentally appropriate skill to begin teaching 2 year old children and teach toward mastery for children 6 years old and up.

Bible Usage: <u>Share</u> is used only 9 times in the Bible, but <u>give</u> is found 1,488 times.

Proverbs 22:9
...for he shares his food with
the poor.

Lesson 2

Opening Prayer: Father God, please be with us today as we learn how to <u>obey</u>. We need to learn how to <u>obey</u> You and our parents.

Scripture: Ephesians 6:1 *Children, <u>obey</u> your parents as the Lord wants, because this is the right thing to do.*

Vocabulary: <u>obey, honor, respect, love</u>

Songs: <u>Children Obey Your Parents</u>, The Wonder Kids, *Mother Goose Bible Songs, Vol. 1*
<u>Trust and Obey</u>, The Wonder Kids, *Bible Songs Sing Alongs*

Snack: Listen and <u>Obey</u>: give kids a small pack of M&M's and eat only what told to eat while playing like Simon Says. Eat one orange M&M, etc.

Story: <u>We Learn to Obey,</u> Ruby and Eli were playing trains. Ruby was getting hungry and wanted some cereal. Ruby's mom gave her some cereal. Ruby didn't eat breakfast and her mom wanted her to eat cereal. Eli saw Ruby eating cereal and wanted some, too. Eli's mom said, "No, you cannot have cereal, Eli. We are going to eat pancakes with grandma." Ruby <u>obeyed</u> her mother and ate her cereal. Eli had to <u>obey</u> his mom and NOT eat cereal. We have to mind our moms and dads. It is the right thing to do! God also gives us rules to follow. He wants us to learn to <u>obey</u> His rules. He wants us to learn to respect other people who are in charge and have rules. Teachers, Church leaders, and grandparents are people who are in charge and have rules. We all learn to listen carefully and <u>obey</u> directions and rules.

Large Motor: Bean Bag Toss: Play like Simon Says. Toss bean bag up, down, over your elbow, under your leg, on top of your foot, etc. The children show how to 'obey'.

Fine Motor: Family Puppets: explore and experiment with the family puppets (prepare in advance with actual photos of each child's family members, or use puppets provided for this activity)

Activity: Mommie, Daddy and ME puppets

Role Play: Mommie tells me to stand up, I <u>obey</u> and stand up
Daddy tells me to sit down, I <u>obey</u> and sit down
Mommie tells me to give daddy a kiss, I <u>obey</u> and give daddy a kiss
Daddy tells me to walk with mommie, I <u>obey</u> and walk with mommie

Close in Prayer: Thank You, Father for my family. Thank You for teaching me to <u>obey</u> my parents. Amen

Parent Guidance: # Obey

Scripture: Ephesians 6:1, *Children, <u>obey</u> your parents as the Lord wants, because this is the right thing to do.*

Ways to <u>Obey</u>: Parents as you begin to teach the concept of <u>obeying</u> to your child, (it's the right thing to do), *do not* fall into the 'trap' of bribing and rewarding. Be creative, because this is very important for your child's development. If a child expects payment for everything that's asked of him, power struggles between parent and child will begin. By avoiding bribing and rewarding, your child will learn self-discipline which is a vital skill lacking in much of today's youth and young adults.

1. Take your child's hand and do the act of <u>obeying</u> alongside your child.

2. Thank your child for doing the right thing.

3. Children can be reasoned with at a much earlier age than we often think possible. This is also the teaching tool desired for logical thinking needed throughout their lives.

Family Puppets: Family puppets with the word <u>obey</u> written on the back of the parents are coming home today. Practice role playing how the child <u>obeys</u> the parents.

Songs Used Today:

<u>Children Obey Your Parents</u>, The Wonder Kids, *Mother Goose Bible Songs, Vol. 1*
<u>Trust and Obey</u>, The Wonder Kids, *Bible Songs Sing Alongs*

Vocabulary Builder: <u>obey, honor, respect, love, trust</u>

Teaching Tidbit: How many times does something need to be done or repeated before it is 'learned' or done by memory? A vague, but easy answer is 20-400! We all learn at different rates, with different abilities and variations. The point is: parents must be patient. Be willing to go the distance in repeating the task that the child is to learn by modeling it over and over. By understanding this learning information, parents can avoid conflicts with their child.

Bible Usage: <u>Obey</u> is found 115 times in the Bible.

Ephesians 6:1
Children, obey your
parents....

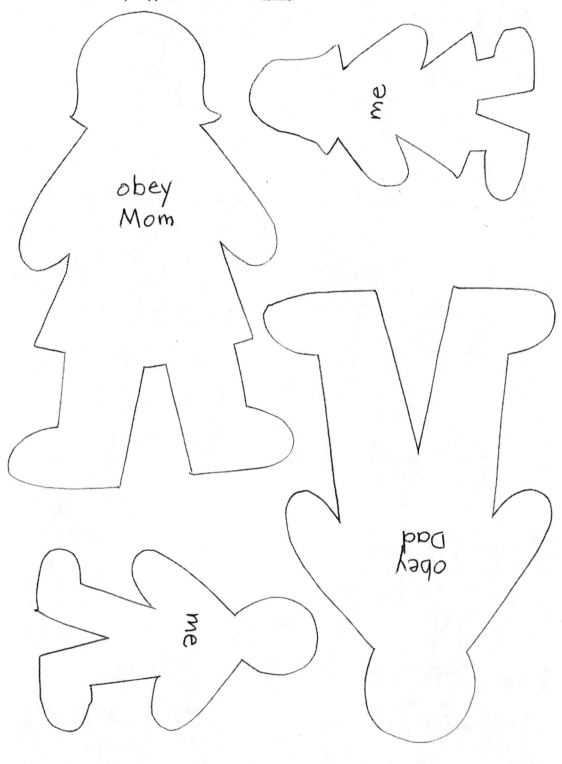

Lesson 3

Opening Prayer: Dear Father, Thank You for <u>forgiving</u> us when we do wrong. Please help us learn to <u>forgive</u> others. Amen

Scripture: Psalm 130:4 *But you <u>forgive</u> us, (so you are respected.)*

Vocabulary: <u>forgive, forgiving, forgiven</u>

Songs: <u>Stephen: Forgive, Forgive</u>, The Wonder Kids, *20 Bible Heroes Vol. 5*

Snack: <u>Forgive</u> our Mess: make messy sandwiches, (kids help spread their own peanut butter) Use cookie cutters to make shape sandwiches, clean up our mess, pour own juice

Story: <u>I Made a Mess</u>, Shane and Eli played blocks in Shane's room. They played with big blocks and little blocks. They played with red blocks and blue blocks. Eli dumped out green blocks. Shane dumped out orange blocks. Then the boys decided they wanted to play with yellow blocks, too. When Shane and Eli were finished playing with blocks, the room was a mess! Shane looked at Eli and said, "I made a mess." Eli looked at Shane and said, "I made a mess, too!" Shane's mom came into the room and saw the mess. Shane looked at Mom and said, "I'm sorry, Mommie. I made a mess." Mom said, "Boys, it's ok to make a mess. We can clean it up." God <u>forgives</u> us when we make a mess. God <u>forgives</u> us when we make a mistake, and ask Him to <u>forgive</u> us. His <u>forgiveness</u> cleans up our mess!

Activity: Teach Me to <u>Forgive</u>: what if I still feel mad? What if my mom makes me say, "I'm sorry." What if someone won't <u>forgive</u> me? What does <u>forgiveness</u> feel like?

Large Motor: Work it Out: Act out the story as it's read the second time through, build with blocks, and clean up the mess

Close in Prayer: Father God, You are love. You love us. You <u>forgive</u> us when we make mistakes. You <u>forgive</u> us when we make a mess. Thank You, Father, for giving us your Son, Jesus. Thank You and Jesus for cleaning up our mess! Amen

Parent Guidance: <u>**Forgive**</u>

Scripture: Psalm 130:4

But you forgive us, (so you are respected.) Or... But with you there is <u>*forgiveness*</u>

Ways to Teach <u>Forgiveness</u>:

1. Model for your child how to pray, talk to God

2. Model for your child how to ask for <u>forgiveness</u>

3. Model for your child how to thank God for His many blessings

4. Model for your child how to have a relationship with God

5. Model actions that need <u>forgiveness</u>

Songs Used Today:

<u>Stephen: Forgive, Forgive</u>, The Wonder Kids, *20 Bible Heroes Vol. 5*

Vocabulary Builder: <u>forgive, forgiven, forgiving</u>

Teaching Tidbit:

If we are to bring God's Kingdom from Heaven to Earth, it is more important for children to learn to have a relationship with God, than to learn rituals within a religion. Our Father is longing for each of us to have a daily relationship with Him. Informal, constant conversation with our "Daddy" is an entirely different way of 'praying'. We can 'clean up our mess' daily by talking to our wonderful Father and asking for <u>forgiveness.</u>

Bible Usage: <u>Forgive</u> is found 95 times in the Bible.

Psalm 130:4
But with you there
is forgiveness

Lesson 4

Opening Prayer: Thank You Father for <u>loving</u> us. Thank You for sharing all things with us. Be with us as we learn to <u>love</u> others.

Scripture: 1 John 3:17-18, *But if anyone has the world's goods and sees his brother in need, yet closes his heart against him, how does God's <u>love</u> abide in him? Little children, let us not <u>love</u> in word or talk, but in deed and in truth.*

Vocabulary: <u>love, caring, sharing, helping others</u>

Songs: <u>This Little Light of Mine</u>, Wonder Kids, *30 Bible Songs and Stories*
        <u>I've Got the Joy, Joy, Joy,</u> Wonder Kids, *30 Bible Songs and Stories*

Snack: Picnic Munchies: put down red and white checked cloth, sit on the floor together, set out picnic snacks of peanut butter sandwiches, carrots, celery and juice, or ants on a log (celery with peanut butter and raisins for ants)

Story: <u>Caring and Sharing = Love,</u> Eli and Ruby went on a picnic. They were in the park with slides and swings. They liked to play in the park with their grandma. Ruby and Eli went down the slide. They giggled and laughed. Then they ran around to go back up the steps to the slide. Sitting beside the slide on the ground was a little boy. The little boy was crying. Ruby and Eli worried about the little boy. Ruby said, "Why are you crying?" The little boy looked up at Ruby. He rubbed his tummy. He said, "My tummy is hungry. My mommie doesn't have any food for me." Ruby looked at Eli. Eli looked at Ruby. Then both Ruby and Eli ran to their grandma. "Grandma, Grandma", Eli and Ruby cried. "We found a hungry boy. He doesn't have any food.

His mommie doesn't have any food, either." Grandma gave both kids a big hug. She said, "I know what we should do. We should give him our picnic. We have more food at home. He can take this food home to share with his mommie." Ruby and Eli were so excited! They ran over to tell the little boy the good news. He stopped crying right away. He gave Ruby and Eli a little hug and ran home with his picnic basket. Grandma gave her grandkids another hug. I'm so proud of you for doing what God would want you to do. He wants us to <u>love</u> others by feeding people who are hungry!

Activity: Fingerprint Ant Art: stamp red and white tablecloth. Weave a tablecloth or glue food cut from magazines in a picnic basket. Fingerprint ants on tablecloth.

Large Motor: Animal Picnic: hop like a bunny, crawl like an ant, fly like a bird, climb like a lizard, swim like a fish, walk like a fox, slither like a snake

Close in Prayer: Dear Father God, Thank You for your <u>love</u>. Thank You for teaching us to <u>love</u> others. I <u>love</u> You, God! Amen

Guidance for Parents: # Love

Scripture: 1 John 3:17-18, *But if anyone has the world's goods and sees his brother in need, yet closes his heart against him, how does God's <u>love</u> abide in him? Little children, let us not <u>love</u> in word or talk, but in deed, and in truth.*

Ways to Model <u>Love</u>:

Let your child be involved in donations to the food bank.
Let your child be involved in tithing.
Give your child coins to bring to Kids of the Kingdom to give to the hungry.
Model <u>love</u> to your child
Model <u>love</u> to your family pet
Model <u>love</u> to family members

Songs used today:

<u>This Little Light of Mine</u>, Wonder Kids, *30 Bible Songs and Stories*
<u>I've Got the Joy, Joy, Joy</u>, Wonder Kids, *30 Bible Songs and Stories*

Vocabulary Builder: <u>caring, sharing, love, helping others</u>

Teaching Tidbit: <u>Caring</u> comes from the heart. Young children, (ages 1-8), are egocentric. Their entire world view is as it pertains to themselves. Children have to be carefully directed to be kind to others and not to 'grab' what they want from others. If really young children are playing with others, they will each be playing by themselves or for themselves. They are not actively playing with each other without 'coaching' from adults or developmental readiness.

Bible Usage: <u>Love</u> is found 547 times in the Bible.

1 John 3:17-18
But whoever has this world's goods, and sees his brother in need...

Lesson 5   2-6 year olds

Opening Prayer: Dear Father God, Thank You for your love. Thank You for loving us <u>forever</u>! Amen

Scripture: Psalm 136, *His love endures <u>forever</u>. Oh give thanks to the LORD; for He is good, His mercy endures <u>forever</u>*

Vocabulary: <u>forever, thanks</u>

Songs: <u>His Love Endures Forever</u>, by Joey G, *A Double Dose*

Story: <u>Forever,</u> Shane heard a song on the radio. It had a catchy tune. He began to sing along. *<u>Forever</u>, and <u>ever</u>, and <u>ever</u>, and <u>ever</u>...* (Sing to tune of Hallelujah Chorus) Ruby and Eli started singing the song, too. Ruby's mom heard her singing the song, <u>Forever</u>. Mom laughed and said, "<u>Forever</u> is a VERY long time. I will love you <u>forever</u>, Ruby. I will love you today, and tomorrow, and the next day, and the next day, and every day after that. My love for you will never stop. I will love you <u>forever</u>!" God loves us <u>forever</u>. He wants us to love Him <u>forever</u>. He wants us to follow His commandments and live with Him <u>forever</u>. That is our purpose. That is our daily job, to love God <u>forever</u>!

Fine Motor: '<u>Forever</u>' Beaded Necklace: String Fruit Loops cereal into a necklace. Talk about the colors and tastes. Talk about how the necklace goes on and on...as a circle goes on <u>forever</u>, the necklace never stops.

Snack: Fruit Loops and milk

Large Motor: Hula Hoops: use one to show how a circle goes on <u>forever</u>. Hold in two hands and slide around and around to show it never ends. Have a hula hoop for each child to explore and move around with.

Activity: <u>Forever</u> Booklets: *God loves us today, tomorrow, the next day, the next day, and the next day, God's love never stops. It goes on <u>forever</u>.* Kids can illustrate their own booklets.

Close in Prayer: Thank You, Father, for loving us <u>forever</u>! Thank You for our parents, our family, our friends. Amen

Guidance for Parents: **<u>Forever</u>**

Scripture: Psalm 136 *His love endures <u>forever</u>. Oh give thanks to the LORD; for He is good, His mercy endures <u>forever</u>*

Ways to Reinforce <u>Forever</u>:

Review the booklet kids made during Kids of the Kingdom time.
Talk about Love with your child. (who, what, when, where, why)
Find the word love in your child's Bible.
Write the word love and put it on your mirror or on the child's bedroom wall.
Discuss: God is love... 1 John 4:8
God says to love others... 1 John 4:7
God's love never ends... Lamentations 3:22-23
God's love endures <u>forever</u>...Psalm 136 (repeat)

Songs used today: <u>His Love Endures Forever</u>, by Joey G, *A Double Dose*

Vocabulary Builder: <u>forever</u>, thanks, love

Teaching Tidbit: Parents have unconditional love for their children. Even when children purposely choose to do wrong, parents are frustrated with the action and the choice, but continue to love their child. God works the same way, only He's perfect in His love, and we have to work to achieve this. Begin to 'open the door' for communication for your children. Children have to be encouraged to visit with their parents about decisions they have to make, things they have done wrong, progress they've made, etc. Open communication at the youngest ages will 'set the stage' for upcoming, more difficult years with your children.

Bible Usage: <u>For ever</u> is found 447 times in the Bible.

Psalm 136
His love endures
forever.

<u>God's Love is Forever</u>

God loves us today,
tomorrow and the next day.

God loves us the next day,
the next day and the next day.

God loves us the next day,
too.

God's love never stops.

His love goes on forever.

Cut 4 inch by 4 inch squares and glue words on each page, leaving room for illustrating.

Honor

Lesson 6

Opening Prayer: Dear Father, Please be with us today as we learn about <u>honor</u> as You want it to be in your Kingdom.

Scripture: *1 Peter 2:17, <u>Honor</u> all people. Love the brotherhood. Fear God. <u>Honor</u> the king.*

Vocabulary: <u>honor</u>

Songs: <u>Children Obey Your Parents</u>, The Wonder Kids, *Mother Goose Bible Songs*

      <u>Life, Righteousness and Honor,</u> Bible Truth Music, *Bible Songs for Kids #7*

      <u>This Little Light of Mine</u>, The Wonder Kids, *30 Songs and 30 Stories*

Snack: Candlelight Snack: string cheese with a mandarin orange on top to look like a candle

Tell the children that the snack looks like a candle. A candle gives us light. We are going to talk about light. Turn off the lights and give each child a battery operated candle for a candlelight snack.

Story: <u>A Room Full of Honor,</u> When Eli stood up, his chair tipped over. Ruby picked it up for Eli. Grandma said, "Thank you, Ruby for showing Eli <u>honor</u>! You treated him special because he needed help. Eli liked hearing his grandma talk about <u>honor</u>. It sounded like such an important word. He looked around the room. There were toys on the floor. Eli walked over to the toys and picked them up. He put them in grandma's toy box. "Here, Grandma!" Eli looked at Grandma expectantly. Grandma was so excited to see what Eli had done. She gave Eli a hug and told him thank you for picking up the toys. "Use the honor word, Grandma." Grandma smiled and said, "Thank you, Eli for showing me honor by picking up the toys!" God is so special to us that we should show Him honor in all that we do. We help others because they are special to God. God created every person on the Earth! They are all special to Him. When you show honor to God's people, you are showing honor to Him.

Fine Motor: Honor Art: color a page to give to someone to show you honor them Be sure to place crayons in the middle of the table to allow kids to show honor by sharing

Large Motor: Balloon Volleyball: each child has a balloon to try to keep in the air. It's good to show honor by helping other children keep their balloons in the air, too.

Activity: Honor Lights: Give children tin cans, small boxes, battery operated candles, and flashlights, to explore light and darkness. Show the children how our light is God living in us, which is good. We want the good to shine in the darkness. Turn off the light, show a can with holes in it, and how it begins to light the darkness. Bring out the light! Hide in the dark with the light and play hide and seek. When we do our very best, we show God's light to others. By showing God's light to others, we are showing God, honor.

Close in Prayer: Dear Father, We love You and show You honor. We honor You, the king! Amen

Guidance for Parents: **Honor**

Scripture: *1 Peter 2:17, <u>Honor</u> all people. Love the brotherhood. Fear God. <u>Honor</u> the king.*

Teachable Moments:

*<u>Honoring</u> the king: The most important lesson in learning honor is to fully respect and 'fear' God. We give Him the highest priority in our lives. Learning His word, means to read and learn the Bible. Following His commandments means to live the life God purposed us for.

*Love the brotherhood, means to have brotherly love for those with whom you worship God. Treat each of them as special. <u>Honor</u> those in leadership roles.

*'<u>Honor</u> all people' means to respect or treat them as being special, because they were specially created by God. God views them as special!

*Teach your child to go beyond what's expected of them. Do extra in <u>honor</u> of the person asking you to do a task. (job)

*Teach your child to say, "Okay" even when they would rather argue about the task being asked of him. Saying okay and doing it shows <u>honor</u>.

Additional Activity: *The way parents show <u>honor</u> to each other and others on a daily basis, becomes the role model that children will learn and demonstrate. Use <u>honor</u> in your statements to your child. "I made you cookies, because I wanted to <u>honor</u> you." "Thank you for showing <u>honor</u> to your daddy, by doing what your daddy asked you to do..."

*When disciplining your child, be sure to convey that the behavior was bad, but the child is good. Your child is a good person who made a bad choice. God loves all the time, and God forgives.

Ways to Model Honor: *Stand to show respect when elderly people enter the room.

*Greet people as they enter the room.

*Stand and place hand over heart for Flag Salute.

*Take hats and caps off inside buildings.

*Say thank you to veterans for their service.

Bible Usage: Honor is found in the Bible 190 times, spelled honour.

1 Peter 2:17
Honour all men...
Honour the King.

Lesson 7

Opening <u>Prayer</u>: Dear Daddy in Heaven, Today we want to learn how to <u>pray</u> to You. We want to learn how to <u>pray</u> without ceasing. We want to thank You, tell You our needs, our joys, our sorrows and our fears. We want to talk to You. Amen

Scripture: Jeremiah 33:3, *Call to me and I will answer you, and show you great and mighty things, which you do not know.*

Vocabulary: <u>pray, ask, answer, ceasing</u>

Songs: <u>We Should Pray</u>, The Wonder Kids, *Bible Songs to Build Confidence*
    <u>I Like to Pray,</u> Various Artists, *25 Bible Action Songs*

Snack: Horn of Plenty: use a waffle cone filled with fresh fruit bites and relate to the cornucopia which is a horn of plenty. Point out to kids that we are <u>praying</u> our thankfulness for food.

Story: <u>I Want to Learn to Pray,</u> Shane told his daddy he wanted to learn how to <u>pray</u>. Shane's daddy was excited to teach Shane to <u>pray</u>. He told Shane to call on God as He is our heavenly Father. We can call Him Daddy, God, Jesus, Father, or many other names used in the Bible. When we call on God, we can begin to talk to Him. We can talk to Him just like we talk to our daddies on Earth. We can tell him our joys, our needs, what makes us sad, or what makes us thankful or fearful. We should always tell Him thank you. It is easy to talk to God, because He loves us so much. He already knows us before we even start to talk to Him. He loves to hear from us. It is easy to talk to God many times a day. If we talk to God all day long, it is called <u>praying</u> without ceasing. That is what God desires. He wants us to talk to Him all day long. If we talk to God all day long, we will have a wonderful relationship with God, our Heavenly Father! Now Shane knows he has two fathers. Jerome is his earthly daddy, and God is his Heavenly Father!

Fine Motor: Prayer Box – cut photos out of magazines or use small items to place in the box if we are thankful for those items. (Food, parents, pets, cars, etc.) Use lunch bags or check boxes if each child is to keep their own.

Large Motor: Pom Pom Prayer Toss: Have a bucket and several pom poms. Each child takes turns saying something they could pray to God about and then toss the pom pom in the bucket.

Activity: Fun Fizz Activity: use Alka Seltzer in colored water to show how excited God feels when we start praying.

Close in Prayer: Father God, thank You for listening to my prayers! I want to talk to You every day! Amen

Guidance for Parents: **Pray**

Scripture: Jeremiah 33:3, *Call to me and I will answer you, and show you great and mighty things, which you do not know.*

Model <u>Praying</u>:

*Morning, mealtime, bedtime, when thankful, when joyful, when fearful, when hurt, when lonely

*If you are <u>praying</u> for someone else who is ill or needs help (Intercessory <u>Prayer</u>)

*Our conversation with God to form the relationship He desires from us is the outcome we want our children to have, rather than rote <u>prayers</u>, with exception to <u>The Lord's Prayer</u> which is Biblical, Matthew 6:9-13, Luke 11:1

Teachable Moment:

Begin to teach The Lord's <u>Prayer</u> by memory

*All lessons within this <u>prayer</u> are vitally important for your child's life! This <u>prayer</u> consists of a summary of the gospels.

*Begin to memorize <u>The Lord's Prayer</u>, by learning one line at a time. Continue to teach what each line means and recite known parts of the prayer each day.

*Add to the Prayer Box that came home today! Help your child learn what he is thankful for, by cutting out pictures from newspapers or magazines.

Songs used today: <u>We Should Pray</u>, The Wonder Kids, *Bible Songs to Build Confidence*
<u>I Like to Pray,</u> Various Artists, *25 Bible Action Songs*

Vocabulary Builder: <u>pray</u>, ask, answer, ceasing

Bible Usage: <u>Pray</u> is mentioned in the Bible 333 times.

Jeremiah 33:3
Call unto me, and I will
answer you...

Lesson 8

Opening Prayer: Father God, Thank You for living in us. Thank You for being the strength, wisdom and <u>power</u> we can use to help us find our way every day. Amen

Scripture: Ephesians 6:10, *...be strong in the Lord and in His mighty <u>power</u>...* Phillipians 4:13, *I can do all things through Christ who strengthens me*

Vocabulary: <u>power</u>

Songs: <u>My God is so Big</u>, Various Artists, *25 Bible Action Songs*

Snack: <u>Power</u> Bar or Granola Bar: <u>Power</u> bars are full of good things for our body. It gives us strength and energy. Apple juice

Story: <u>God is My Power</u>, Ruby told Shane he was strong. Shane wanted to show Eli just how strong he was, so he tried to pick up his tractor that he rides outside. Shane tried really hard to pick up the tractor. Shane tried again to pick up the tractor. He could not pick up the tractor! Ruby said that Shane was still strong, because God is strong. God lives in Shane! God is all strength, <u>power</u> and might. He lives in each of us. Because God lives in us with all His <u>power</u>, we can access God's <u>power</u> to beat our enemy, the devil. When the devil tries to hurt us, or get us to choose wrong choices, God's strength helps us over <u>power</u> the devil! The devil loses and God wins! We are so thankful that God's <u>power</u> lives in all of us!

Fine Motor: Jesus Calms the Storm with His <u>Power</u>: color the boat and water, and place fish stickers in the water

Activity: Luke 18:27, is a good example to show children about God's <u>power</u> as Jesus performed a miracle and calmed the storm. Make a paper boat, water, and craft stick activity that shows how the water rocked the boat, and how Jesus has the <u>power</u> from God to calm the waters. See following page for patterns.

Large Motor: Simon Says God's Way: God says, jump. God says, shout hooray! God says, touch your shoe. God says, turn in a circle. God says, walk to the door. God says, sit in your chair. All of creation, people and animals do as God says! That is God's <u>power</u>.

Close in Prayer: Dear Father, You are so <u>powerful</u> and mighty. We share your world created by your <u>power</u>. Amen

Guidance for Parents: <u>**Power**</u>

Scripture: Ephesians 6:10, *...be strong in the Lord and in His mighty <u>power</u>...*

Phillipians 4:13, *I can do all things through Christ who strengthens me*

Ways to Help Your Child Understand <u>Power</u>:

*Luke 18:27, is a good example to show children about God's <u>power</u> as Jesus performed a miracle and calmed the storm.

*Go outside at night and look at the sky. Lay in the yard and look at the stars. Talk about how magnificent (amazing, huge) God's creation is. God's creation shows His immense <u>power</u>. Read a story about God's creation, as found in Genesis.

Songs used today: <u>My God is so Big</u>, Various Artists, *25 Bible Action Songs*

Vocabulary Builder: <u>Power</u>

Bible Usage: <u>Power</u> is used in the Bible 383 times.

Ephesians 6:10
...be strong in the Lord and in the power of His might

Use with Jesus Calms the Storm with His Power in Lesson 8 – <u>Power</u>

Cut and glue the image of *Jesus and the Children on the Boat* to a craft stick. Cut the top and bottom of 8 ½ by 11 inch blue paper to look like waves. Fold the blue paper in half unevenly to look like two levels of water. Cut a slit in the fold of the water. The stick will fit inside the fold of the water. Add fish stickers in the water. As the stick is moved, it will appear as though the boat is rocking roughly on the water because the wind and storm are strong. When Jesus uses God's power to calm the storm, the boat stops rocking.

Cut

Cut

8½ by 11 blue

fold

popsicle stick

Lesson 9

Opening Prayer: Dear Father in Heaven, Thank You for loving us. Thank You for teaching us about <u>trusting</u> You. Amen

Scripture: Proverbs 3:5, *Trust in the LORD with all your heart*

Vocabulary: <u>trust</u>

Songs: <u>Trust and Obey</u>, The Wonder Kids, *Bible Songs Sing Alongs*

Snack: Learning to <u>Trust</u>: Show that the kids are <u>trusted</u> to pour their own drink from a pitcher. Spills are acceptable, as we partner together to clean it up. Show kids again that they are <u>trusted</u> to 'smear' their own apple butter on mini waffles and clean up the mess.

Story: <u>Learning to Trust</u>, Church was at Mario's house today. When Shane walked into Mario's house, a GREAT BIG dog walked over to Shane and Ruby. Ruby squealed with delight! But Shane was very nervous to be beside the BIG dog. Shane walked away from the dog, over to his grandad, because he <u>trusted</u> his grandad to keep him safe from the BIG dog. When Church was ready to start, Eli opened the door, and the BIG dog got loose and ran outside. Eli and Mario called and called for the dog, but the dog didn't come home. Everyone started looking for the BIG dog. Shane and his grandad looked for the BIG dog. Shane told his grandad he was worried about the dog. Grandad said, "Well, Shane, let's pray to God that the dog will come back home. We will <u>trust</u> God to bring the dog back home." Shane and his grandad prayed. During worship, Mario and the dog walked in the back door. Shane was so excited, he could hardly contain his joy. He jumped up and down. He squealed with delight. He waved his arms up and down. He understood that God heard his prayer to bring the dog home, and God answered that prayer. Shane learned he could <u>trust</u> God! God is good!

Fine Motor: Touchy-Feely Box: kids show <u>trust</u> as they stick their hands in an unknown, unseen box to feel the items. Can they guess what the item is? Talk about how they can <u>trust</u> the teacher, leader, or parent.

Large Motor: Blind Fold Walk: teacher will help guide kids as they take turns wearing a blind fold. Do you <u>trust</u> the teacher to help you? How does it feel to <u>trust</u>?

Activity: Who Can You <u>Trust</u>? Jump up if it is someone kids can <u>trust,</u> or sit down if it is someone not to <u>trust</u>: Mommie, Daddy, stranger, policeman, man across the street, teacher, lady at the grocery store, older kid in the park, etc.

Close in Prayer: Thank You dear God for being with us all the time. Thank You for your love. Thank You for teaching us how to <u>trust</u> You in all things. Amen

Guidance for Parents: **<ins>Trust</ins>**

Scripture: Proverbs 3:5, *<ins>Trust</ins> in the LORD with all your heart*

Teachable Moment: Teach your child that sometimes it doesn't look like prayers get answered. Ex: Your child said a prayer asking for a big, new bike like a friend has. Maybe your child provided the perfect opportunity to learn that God hears **<ins>every</ins>** prayer. But we might not get what we prayed for. Sometimes He has better plans for us. Sometimes He chooses to answer our prayer request, but He chooses the timing and we might have to wait a long time. We need to learn to pray in thankfulness, worship, praise, for others, and not for items we wish we could have. So here's the hard part of <ins>trusting</ins> God, <ins>trusting</ins> Him enough to know that His answer is the best answer for us! Not what our soul is asking for, like that fancy new bike.

Songs used today: <ins>Trust and Obey</ins>, The Wonder Kids, *Bible Songs Sing Alongs*

Vocabulary Builder: <ins>trust</ins>

Bible Usage: The word <ins>trust</ins> is used in the Bible 169 times.

Proverbs 3:5
Trust in the LORD
with all your heart.

Lesson 10

Opening Prayer: Thank You Father for giving us <u>hope.</u> <u>Hope</u>, and a future through your Son, Jesus Christ. Amen

Scripture: 1 Peter 1:3, *He has given us new birth into a living <u>hope</u> through the resurrection of Jesus Christ from the dead (Easter)*

Vocabulary: <u>hope</u>, resurrection

Songs: <u>Jesus Loves Me</u>

Snack: Butterfly Food Art: fresh fruit and cheese chunks in the shape of a butterfly

Story: <u>The Hope of the Caterpillar,</u> The <u>hope</u> of the caterpillar is to find new life. Each little caterpillar has the <u>hope</u> of becoming a beautifully transformed butterfly in his lifetime. First, a butterfly lays an egg. The egg lies on a leaf to grow. Next, the egg hatches into a caterpillar. The caterpillar grows up in the world by eating leaves and crawling around. When the caterpillar is fully grown, he crawls up on a leaf and turns himself into a crysallis. He completely covers himself in a blanket. After being kept warm and safe in the blanket, he begins to hatch out of the crysallis. When he is born again, he is a beautiful butterfly! Isn't God's creation of the butterfly amazing? He did the same thing with his *Son,* Jesus! Jesus was born a tiny new baby, just like us. When Jesus was grown up, he died. They wrapped Him in blankets and put Him in a safe place, called a tomb. After three days, He was born again! He rose again, and lives in heaven with God the Father, and lives everywhere on Earth, and He lives in our hearts! God's plan of <u>Hope</u> is truly amazing!

> The <u>Hope</u> of Jesus is that He rose from the dead and HE lives!
> He lives in heaven with God, His father.
> He lives in our hearts!
> He lives everywhere!

Fine Motor: Resurrection Story Sequencing Booklet: see worksheet

Large Motor: Charades: The <u>Hope</u> of New Life, butterfly life cycle.

Jesus and The Resurrection, life, buried in a tomb, come to life, live in heaven and everywhere!

Activity: What Do You <u>Hope</u> For? What would a dog <u>hope</u> for? What would a tiger <u>hope</u> for? What <u>hopes</u> do you have? What <u>hopes</u> do your parents have? If photos or graphics can be found, make a concentration game in advance.

Close in Prayer: Dear Father, With You we have <u>hope</u>. With your Son, Jesus, we have <u>hope</u> for a life and a future. Thank You, Amen

Guidance for Parents: # Hope

Scripture: 1 Peter 1:3, *He has given us new birth into a living* <u>*hope*</u> *through the resurrection of Jesus Christ from the dead (Easter)*

Teachable Moment:

> Jesus rose from the dead and HE lives!
> He lives in heaven with God, His father.
> He lives in our hearts!
> He lives everywhere!

*Review the Lesson from Today: What Do You <u>Hope</u> For?

*Review the three page Resurrection lesson also coming home today.

*Charades: The <u>Hope</u> of New Life, butterfly life cycle.

*Jesus and The Resurrection, life, buried in a tomb, come to life, live in heaven and everywhere!

Songs used today: <u>Jesus Loves Me</u>

Vocabulary Builder: <u>hope</u>, resurrection

Bible Usage: The word <u>hope</u> is used in the Bible 156 times.

1 Peter 1:3
He has given us new
birth into a living hope..

Use with <u>Resurrection Story Sequencing Booklet</u> in Lesson 10- <u>Hope</u>

Jesus Died for My Sins

Resurrection Story Sequencing Booklet

Jesus died on the cross for my sins.

>>>

He was buried, but came back to life.

>>>

He lives in Heaven with God the Father, and in my heart!

Lesson 11

Opening Prayer: Dear Father, Thank You for being our Father and giving us <u>faith</u> and your promise. We know that You have our worries and we can believe You will take care of us in all things. Teach us to have <u>faith</u>, even if we cannot see it with our eyes.

Scripture: Corinthians 5:7, *...we walk by <u>faith</u>, not by sight*

Vocabulary: <u>faith</u>

Songs: <u>Have Faith in God</u>, LifeWay Kids, *Worship Kidstyle*

Snack: <u>F</u>aith of a Mustard Seed: find the smallest clay pots and wash them thoroughly. Fill with applesauce. Add cheese stick with top cut at a slant. Sit arrowroot cookie shaped like a flower on the cheese stick. Place raspberry in center of cookie.

Story: <u>Planting a Garden</u>, Grandad and Shane knew the weather was getting nicer. The sun was warmer, and it rained some. Grandad told Shane it was time to plant a garden. Shane wanted to plant beans, peas and corn. Grandad wanted to plant cucumbers, tomatoes and pumpkins. Grandad got the ground ready in the garden spot. He raked the ground. He made little holes in the dirt, and let Shane put in the seeds. Shane liked looking at the seeds. They were so little. They all looked different. Shane put the seeds in the holes and Grandad covered them with dirt. Shane and Grandad watered the seeds and left them alone. When Grandad and Shane went back to check the seeds the next day, nothing had changed. There was nothing there! When Shane and Grandad went back two days later, a couple of little green stems were coming up! When Shane and Grandad went back every day after that, they saw the plants growing and changing. The plants were beginning to grow beans, peas, corn, pumpkins, cucumbers and tomatoes! This is like a prayer. We pray to God, and <u>trust</u> Him. We wait on God to answer the prayer in His way and in His timing. It might take a day, a week or longer, but we wait with <u>faith</u>. We know God will answer our prayer if we have <u>faith</u>. If we have <u>faith</u> even as tiny as the mustard seed, we can do so much with God and His awesome power! We don't have to see it to believe it!

Activity: Seed Discovery: use seeds such as watermelon seeds and sunflower seeds that children might be familiar with to show and tell. Allow time for children to "guess".

Fine Motor: Growing <u>Faith</u>: plant marigold seeds in pots. Add water. Predict what the seeds will do. Talk about how fast they'll grow. Compare to <u>faith</u> the size of a mustard seed. If we have <u>faith</u> only the size of the smallest seed, we can move mountains if we partner with God and His amazing power! Show dirt in a planter, newly planted seed, or newly asked prayer. Show small sprout in a planter, a planted seed a short time ago, prayer being answered. Show blooming plant in a planter, prayer asked a while ago, and compare to waiting for God's timing. We don't have to see to believe!

Large Motor: <u>Faith</u>walk: wearing blindfolds, try to pin the flower on the flower pot... spin three times and try to find the flower pot without help. Then try again with the guidance of the teacher (God) showing the way to find the desired result of the prayer. Pin the flower on the flower pot. Relate to today's scripture, Corinthians 5:7, *We walk by <u>faith</u>, not by sight.*

Close in Prayer: Dear Father, It is so amazing that we can turn our prayers over to You, and trust that You will take care of us all the time! Help us grow our <u>faith</u> in You! Amen

Guidance for Parents: # Faith

Scripture: Corinthians 5:7, *...we walk by <u>faith</u>, not by sight*

Ways to Teach <u>Faith</u>:

Practice and model praying and waiting on God with your child.
Teach your child to wait on the LORD.
Revisit this often to allow your child to see the prayers come to fruition.

Teachable Moment:

<u>Faith</u> is the absence of fear. Does your child have nighttime fears or other worries that can be used in this lesson? Practice laying these fears at the Father's feet and growing in confidence and <u>faith</u> that there is no need for fear. God has us in His care and will take care of us forever. (That doesn't guarantee we won't have hardships in our lives, BUT it does guarantee that He'll remain <u>faithful</u> in seeing us through those hardships!)

Songs used today: <u>Have Faith in God</u>, LifeWay Kids, *Worship Kidstyle*

Vocabulary Builder: <u>faith</u>

Bible Usage: <u>Faith</u> is used 242 times in the Bible.

Corinthians 5:7
...we walk by faith,
not by sight

Use with Faith of a Mustard Seed in Lesson 11 - Faith

Lesson 12

Opening Prayer: Thank You Father for sending us your Son, Jesus. Jesus is the greatest gift ever given! He is the way, the <u>truth</u>, and the life. We welcome Jesus to live in us and direct our lives. Amen

Scripture: John 14:6, *Jesus said to him, "I am the way, and the <u>truth</u> and the life; no one comes to the Father but through Me."*

Vocabulary: <u>truth</u>

Songs: <u>Every Move I Make</u>, Totally Kids Worship, *Everyday*

Snack: Slimy Snake Snack: In the Bible, evil became a snake and told lies. Do not believe lies! We are going to make a slimy snake, and eat it! We won't believe his lies! Cut a Twinkie or Jelly Roll horizontally, and lay it end to end. Cut a point to the head and place two triangles on top for the head. Use licorice for tongue and fruit to decorate.

Story: Preface our story with: God loves Jesus, Jesus loves God

John 3:16 *For God so loved the world that He gave His only begotten Son, that whosoever believeth in Him should not perish, but have everlasting life.*

<u>Look for Truth</u>, by Kim Lyon, The world is good. God created a beautiful planet full of goodness. But sadly, there is bad in God's world, too. There is evil, and evil is BAD! We want to stay away from evil. This is like a big fight for you every day. John 14:6 In the Bible Jesus says, "I am the way, and the truth and the life; no one comes to the Father but through Me."

Every day we look for Jesus. Jesus is the happy way. Jesus is the good way, making good choices. Jesus makes us feel joyful and happy. Jesus is the truth. Evil tells us lies. Evil tells us bad things. Evil tells us to make bad choices. If it feels dark and sad, look for the truth. Jesus is the truth! It says so in the Bible. If we believe in God, and His son, Jesus, and look for the truth in all things, we belong to God's kingdom. We will find the way, the truth and the life with God in Heaven and on Earth!! Yay, for truth!

Fine Motor: Truth Toss: each child needs a muffin tin, a few large pom poms and truths about Jesus. (Or play as a group. See following page.) The muffin tin sections will each have a phrase. If the phrase is true, the kids yell, "Truth!" If it is not truth, yell, "Lie!"

Large Motor: It's the Truth: like Simon Says. If the teacher says, "My shirt is red," and it is red, the children stand up and yell, "Truth." If the teacher says something that is untrue, the children sit down. Be obvious with directions. (I am a boy, I have a mommie, I am going down a slipper slide, I am in a car, etc.)

Close in Prayer: Dear Jesus, Please walk beside us every day and help us learn to hear the truth. Help us know when it is a lie, and to turn toward the truth. Amen

Guidance for Parents: <u>**Truth**</u>

Scripture: John 14:6 *Jesus said to him, "I am the way, and the <u>truth</u> and the life; no one comes to the Father but through Me."*

Teachable Moment:

<u>Truth</u> is <u>true, just...</u>

It is important to tell the <u>truth</u>.

Teach the roles of Jesus and God, Father and Son, how much they love each other.

The Bible says we can 'come to the Father, through his Son, Jesus.'

- If we believe in Jesus, we have access to the Father

- The whole Bible is based on God's Son, Jesus

- Jesus and God are One

- They also have the Holy Spirit

- All three are One

Read: <u>God, Jesus and The Holy Spirit</u>, by Kim Lyon

Songs used today: <u>Every Move I Make</u>, Totally Kids Worship, *Everyday*

Vocabulary Builder: <u>truth</u>

Bible Usage: The word <u>truth</u> is used in the Bible 263 times.

John 14:6
Jesus said, "I am the way, the truth and the life."

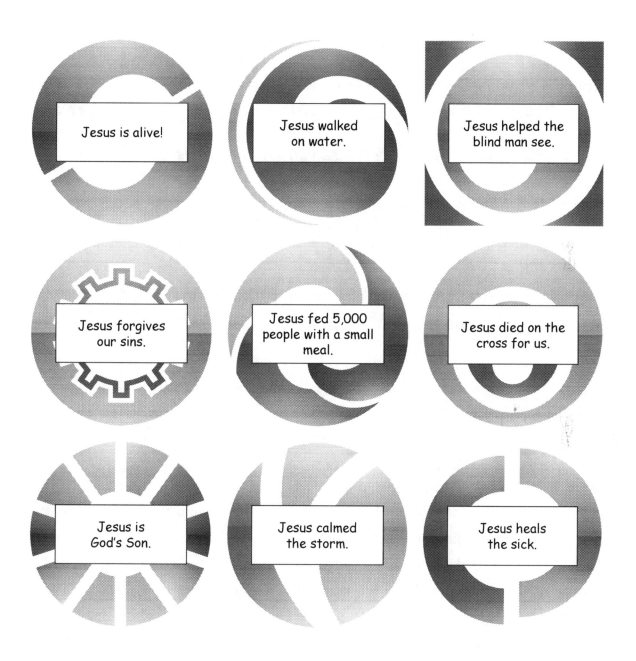

Jesus is alive!

Jesus walked on water.

Jesus helped the blind man see.

Jesus forgives our sins.

Jesus fed 5,000 people with a small meal.

Jesus died on the cross for us.

Jesus is God's Son.

Jesus calmed the storm.

Jesus heals the sick.

Lesson 13

Opening Prayer: Dear Father God, We praise You for sending us your Son, Jesus. We love to praise You with dancing and singing! Amen

Scripture: Psalms 138:1, *I will praise you with my whole heart...*

Vocabulary: praise

Songs: I'm Happy All the Time, The Wonder Kids, *30 Bible Songs and 30 Bible Stories*
Praise the Lord, Oh My Soul, Steve Green, *Hide 'em In Your Heart*
He's Got the Whole World In His Hands, Wee Worship, *Favorite Bible Songs*

Snack: Praisins: give each child a waffle and raisins. The children can fill each square with a raisin!

Story: Raise Your Praise, Jerome, Kaley and Ruby were leading worship at Church, and sang, "Raise your praise!" Eli and Shane liked the way these words sounded. They liked the way the music got louder. Hands were clapping and reaching for Jesus. They liked the smiles on their parents' faces. They liked the feeling of wanting to sing, clap and dance. We love to praise! When we praise God, He wants us to praise His Son, Jesus. When we praise Jesus, He wants us to praise His Father, God! They both want us to feel the Holy Spirit dancing and praising inside of us! We can praise the Father, Son and Spirit anytime, anywhere, any way we want to sing, dance, or pray!

Fine Motor: Make musical instruments, dance, and <u>praise</u> and sing!

Shakers: water bottle, rice, or aquarium rocks, hot glue the lid to avoid spills

Ribbon Dancers: use a shower curtain ring and ribbons cut at various lengths, tie the ribbons onto the shower curtain ring

Drum/Tambourines: using two heavy duty paper plates, fill the plates with a few beans and lay a couple of streamers across the inside of the plate. Staple the plates together upside down.

Large Motor: Dance for Joy: show feelings by dancing with movements to music. Wave scarves, ribbons or use shakers to raise the praise, get noisy…. with happiness and joy!

<u>I Exalt Thee</u>, Various Artists, *51 Must Have Worship Songs for Kids*

Close in Prayer: Dear Father God, We <u>praise</u> You! We <u>praise</u> You for being the One, true God. We <u>praise</u> You for being our creator, our provider and our savior! Amen

Guidance for Parents: **Praise**

Scripture: Psalms 138:1 *I will praise you with my whole heart...*

Ways to Teach Praise: There are lots of reasons to praise God, but mostly for His Son, Jesus.

Make musical instruments, dance, praise and sing!

Raise the praise, get noisy.... With happiness and joy!

Teachable Moment:

God delights in His Son, Jesus.
Jesus delights in His Father, God.
God and Jesus share their being with the Holy Spirit.
We find joy in praising God, Jesus and the Holy Spirit.

Share the book: God, Jesus and The Holy Spirit, by Kim Lyon

Songs used today:

I'm Happy All the Time, The Wonder Kids, *30 Bible Songs and 30 Bible Stories*
Praise the Lord, Oh My Soul, Steve Green, *Hide 'em In Your Heart*
He's Got the Whole World In His Hands, Wee Worship, *Favorite Bible Songs*
I Exalt Thee, Various Artists, *51 Must Have Worship Songs for Kids*

Vocabulary Builder: praise

Bible Usage: The word praise is used 248 times in the Bible.

Psalms 138:1
I will praise you with my
whole heart...

Lesson 14

Opening Prayer: Dear Daddy in Heaven, Thank You for giving us your Son, Jesus! Thank You for filling us with <u>joy</u> when we spend time with either of You! Amen

Scripture: Psalm 16:11, ...*in Thy presence is fullness of <u>joy</u>*

Vocabulary: <u>joy</u>

Songs: <u>Joy to the World</u>

<u>I've Got Joy, Joy, Joy, Joy</u>, The Wonder Kids, 30 *Bible Songs and 30 Bible Stories*

<u>Jesus Loves Me</u>, The Wonder Kids, *30 Bible Songs and 30 Bible Stories*

<u>I'm Happy All the Time</u>, The Wonder Kids, *30 Bible Songs and 30 Bible Stories*

<u>This is My Commandment</u>, The Wonder Kids, *30 Bible Songs and 30 Bible Stories*

Snack: <u>Joy</u> Bars: Almond <u>Joy</u> candy bars or bars made of cereal and marshmallow cream

Story: <u>Oh Boy, I Feel Joy!</u>, by Kim Lyon, "Oh boy! I feel joy! I just feel so happy! I just can't help but giggle and dance and wave my arms", exclaimed Shane. His grandma laughed and joined in. They turned on music, a jazzy song, of course, and giggled, and sang out loud, and danced. Grandma and Shane felt happy and full of <u>joy</u>! When our hearts are full of <u>joy</u>, we are full of God, His Son Jesus and His Holy Spirit. All three live in our hearts. All three live in our heads, our spirit, our soul, and our flesh! Everywhere in our bodies, we feel the joy of God! When we are filled with joy, we just can't keep our bodies from dancing! Let's dance!

Fine Motor: Joy to the World: Use bells to play the color coded song of Joy to the World. Bells can be purchased online.

Large Motor: Dancing for Joy! Lots of dancing and praising to share and express our joy to the Lord!

Activity: Nativity Joy: make or display a nativity scene to celebrate our joy at the birth of Jesus Christ our Saviour! Son of God and King of man!

Close in Prayer: Dear Father God, We feel such joy as this time of year we celebrate the birth of your baby Son, Jesus. We thank you that He grew to be a man who died for our sins, salvation, grace and healing! We are filled with joy! Amen

Guidance for Parents: **<u>Joy</u>**

Scripture: Psalm 16:11, *...in Thy presence is fullness of <u>joy</u>*

Ways to Teach <u>Joy</u>:

*Demonstrate personal emotions to your child

*Help them put vocabulary and dialog to what they are feeling

*Draw circles and draw happy faces, sad faces, scared faces, surprised faces, etc. Put them on craft sticks and use as puppets with a story.

*Look up lessons on *The Fruit of the Spirit*

Teachable Moment:

The Holy Spirit gives us <u>joy</u>.....<u>joy</u> is a happy feeling inside of us!

Christmas is the celebration and <u>joy</u> surrounding the birth of Jesus.

Songs used today: <u>Joy to the World</u>,
<u>I've Got Joy, Joy, Joy, Joy</u>, The Wonder Kids, *30 Bible Songs and 30 Bible Stories*
<u>Jesus Loves Me</u>, The Wonder Kids, *30 Bible Songs and 30 Bible Stories*
<u>I'm Happy All the Time</u>, The Wonder Kids, *30 Bible Songs and 30 Bible Stories*
<u>This is My Commandment</u>, The Wonder Kids, *30 Bible Songs and 30 Bible Stories*

Vocabulary Builder: <u>joy</u>

Bible Usage: The word <u>joy</u> is found in the Bible 198 times.

Psalm 16:11
...in Thy presence is
fullness of joy

Joy to the World

8	7	6	5	4	3	2
1	5	6	6	7	7	8
8	8	7	6	5	5	4
3	8	8	7	6	5	5
4	3	3	3	3	3	3
4	5	4	3	2	2	2
2	3	4	3	2	1	8
6	5	4	3	4	3	2
1						

Lesson 15

Opening Prayer: Dear Father God, Thank You for sending Jesus as a person in the <u>flesh</u>. We are excited to learn about Jesus! Amen

Scripture: John 1:14, *And the Word became <u>flesh</u> and dwelt among us.*

Vocabulary: <u>flesh</u>

Songs: <u>He's Got the Whole World In His Hands</u>, Wee Worship, *Favorite Bible Songs*

<u>Jesus Loves the Little Children</u>

Snack: Children of the World: use a boy or gingerbread boy cookie cutter to cut different colors of meat, cheese and bread, to show different colors of <u>flesh</u> on the people of the Earth. Place a sugar cookie in the center, with blue and green frosting to look like the Earth. Place Children of the World all around the Earth. All colors of <u>flesh</u> make up our world!

Story: What is <u>Flesh</u>? <u>Flesh</u> is our skin. All people have <u>flesh</u>. Not all people are the same color. People have different colors of skin. How are people the same? (feelings, families, food, grow, have hair, etc.) How are people different? We have different colors of <u>flesh</u>, different looks, different feelings, etc. Our own desires are called, "of the <u>flesh</u>". It's what our 'body' wants. We want to do what God tells us to do, instead of listening to our own <u>flesh</u>.

Fine Motor: The Many Colors of <u>Flesh</u>: using <u>flesh</u> colored markers, color the bottom of a person or gingerbread boy cookie cutter and stamp it on paper around the world

Large Motor: <u>Flesh</u> of the Earth: form a circle and join hands. Play <u>Ring Around the Rosie</u> while singing to the tune of <u>Here We Go Looby Loo</u>... *Here we go 'round the Earth. Here we go 'round the Earth. Here we go 'round the Earth. Holding hands together.* While singing and holding hands together... raise hands up to the sky. Go the opposite direction each time you sing it. Compare the different colors of <u>flesh</u> on our hands. Trade places and compare <u>flesh</u> again.

Activity: Begin three layer puppet showing <u>flesh</u>, soul and spirit (trace cookie cutter 3 times)

Our skin is called '<u>flesh</u>' (use flesh color for each child)

Soul is our living being, feelings, needs, wants inside of us (use white paper)

Spirit is Jesus as our inner layer (make out of thin paper such as tissue paper)

Close in Prayer: Thank You Father for creating Jesus in spirit and in <u>flesh</u> to come to Earth for us. We love your Son, Jesus! We can learn to pray to Jesus, whom You sent to Earth to be our Lord and King. Amen

Guidance for Parents: # Flesh

Scripture: John 1:14, *And the Word became <u>flesh</u> and dwelt among us, and we have seen his glory, glory as of the only Son from the Father, full of grace and truth.*

Ways to Teach <u>Flesh</u>:

    *<u>Flesh</u> colored crayons, photo of kids around the world to color
    *Paper doll punches or cut outs of kids of all colors, Earth in center, heart on the Earth to represent Jesus
    *Gingerbread boy cookie cutter, watercolor marker or ink pad the bottom and stamp around the edges of the world, using different <u>flesh</u> colors
    *make a collage of people with different <u>flesh</u> colors

Teachable Moment:

While people look different on the outside, we are the same inside. Our skin is called '<u>flesh</u>' Our own desires are called 'of the <u>flesh</u>'. Purchase the book: <u>God, Jesus and The Holy Spirit</u>, by Kim Lyon. God is spirit. Jesus is <u>flesh</u> and spirit. Holy Spirit is spirit. People are <u>flesh</u> and spirit. Jesus was created to relate to us as <u>flesh</u> (bodies and souls). We have Jesus in our lives as a spirit to allow us access to God as spirit.

Songs used today:

    <u>He's Got the Whole World In His Hands,</u> Wee Worship, *Favorite Bible Songs*
    <u>Jesus Loves the Little Children</u>

Vocabulary Builder: <u>flesh</u>

Bible Usage: <u>Flesh</u> is found in the Bible 405 times.

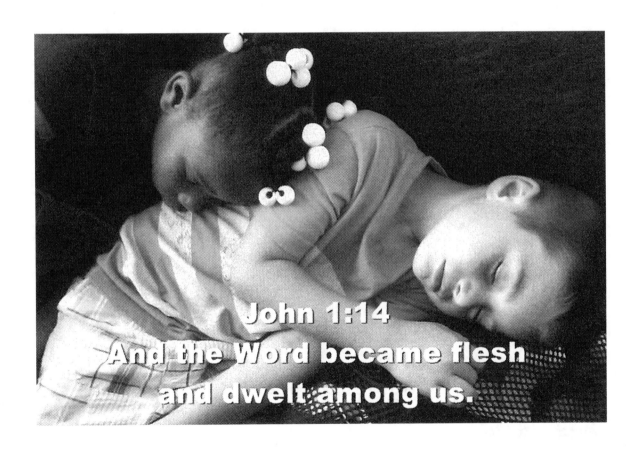

John 1:14
And the Word became flesh
and dwelt among us.

Use with Children of the World Snack in Lesson 15 – <u>Flesh</u>

Use with Colors of Flesh Around the World - <u>Flesh</u>

Lesson 16

Opening Prayer: Dear Father God, Thank You for helping us resist temptation that our <u>souls</u> desire. Sometimes we want to eat too much food. Sometimes we want to take a toy away from a friend. Sometimes we do things we're not supposed to do. Thank You Father for reminding us to do the right thing and not let our <u>souls</u> be in charge! We will come to You. Amen

Scripture: Psalm 121:7, *The LORD shall preserve you from all evil; He shall preserve your <u>soul</u>.*

Vocabulary: <u>Soul</u>

Songs: <u>Rock-A-My Soul</u>, Wee Worship, *Favorite Worship Songs*
       <u>Praise the Lord, Oh My Soul</u>, Steve Green, *Hide 'Em In Your Heart*
       <u>I've Got Peace Like a River</u>, Countdown Kids, *We Worship and Adore*

Snack: <u>Sou</u>licious: strawberries and strawberry candy, baked crackers and chips, grapes and grape jelly, Cheerios and donut, etc. Talk about added sugar being delicious, but not the healthy choice.

Story: <u>Healthy Choices</u>, by Kim Lyon, Every day Shane has to make choices. For breakfast, his mommie made him cereal with milk, but Shane wanted a donut. Shane threw a little fit to get his donut. During playtime, Eli was playing with dinosaurs. Shane wanted to play with dinosaurs, so he walked over and took two dinosaurs from Eli. Eli cried. At lunch, Shane wanted to pour salt on his sandwich. His mommie said not to pour salt on his sandwich, but Shane did it anyway. It tasted awful! Shane played in the sandbox. His mommie said not to throw sand. Shane wanted to throw sand. Soon it was all over Shane's face! Shane was not having a good day. He started to think about the choices he had made. He upset his mommie at breakfast when his <u>soul</u> inside him wanted a donut. He upset Eli at playtime when his <u>soul</u> inside him wanted to take his dinosaurs. He upset his mommie at lunchtime when his <u>soul</u> wanted to pour salt on his sandwich. Shane knew that he had heard about making good choices. But, how do we make good choices? Ask God. We can ask God what we should do, and God will help us make the right choice. God will protect our <u>souls</u> if we follow His commandments, choose right, and give our <u>souls</u> to Him. To give our <u>souls</u> to Him means to do His will instead of our own.

Fine Motor: Three Layer Puppet: the body will be an actual photo of each child or use page of flesh, soul and spirit used in previous lesson. Our body includes our heart, mind, and a covering with skin. We clean our body with bathing. Our <u>soul</u> is part of our living being, it is a breath of God, our feelings, needs, and temptations also inside our body. We clean our <u>soul</u> with prayer and asking God for forgiveness. Our spirit is the third part inside our body, Jesus living inside of us which needs no cleaning!

Activity: Sin Cleanse: Use Dawn soap, oil and water experiment: Have a clear glass of water. Add a capful of cooking oil as the sin or unhealthy choice. Add a drop of Dawn dish soap and watch as "God" cleans up the sin and fixes our <u>souls</u>.

Large Motor: Follow the Leader: Go for a long walk and the leader will do different actions that the kids must follow. After the walk, talk about following others only while making good choices. Say no if the choices are bad!

Close in Prayer: Thank You, Father for always being beside us to help us make healthy choices. You are amazing and You are full of love as we learn to follow You! Amen

Guidance for Parents: **<u>Soul</u>**

Scripture: Psalm 121:7, *The LORD shall preserve you from all evil; He shall preserve your <u>soul.</u>*

Ways to Teach About <u>Souls</u>: God will protect our <u>souls</u> if we follow His commandments, choose right, and give our souls to Him. To give our <u>souls</u> to Him means to do His will instead of our own.

*Create two puppets with your child. One is an Ugly monster called, '<u>Soulman</u>'. One is a nice looking boy or girl to be the child following God's help in making good choices. Play games with the puppets. Give the child scenarios and the child will show which puppet it was. Ex: Ran into the street, ate a good dinner, colored on the walls, sang a song, got dressed, cried for a new toy, etc.

Songs used today: <u>Rock-A-My Soul</u>, Wee Worship, *Favorite Worship Songs*
<u>Praise the Lord, Oh My Soul,</u> Steve Green, *Hide 'Em In Your Heart*
<u>I've Got Peace Like a River</u>, Countdown Kids, *We Worship and Adore*

Vocabulary Builder: <u>Soul</u>

Bible Usage: The word <u>soul</u> is used in the Bible 496 times.

Psalm 121:7 He shall preserve your soul

Lesson 17

Opening Prayer: Dear Father God, Be with us today as we learn who You are. We want to learn your word of <u>law</u> as we read in the Bible. We want to learn your commandments and learn to obey your <u>law</u>. Thank You for loving us! Amen

Scripture: 1 John 2:1-2, *My little children, I am writing <u>these things</u> to you…* 1 Peter 1:24 *But the <u>word</u> of the LORD endures forever*

Vocabulary: <u>law, word, scripture, commandments</u>

Songs: <u>The B I B L E</u>, Wonder Kids, *30 Bible songs and 30 Bible Stories*
<u>This is My Commandment</u>, Wonder Kids, *30 Bible songs and 30 Bible Stories*

Snack: Stoplight Snack: a piece of celery with cream cheese in the center. Use a red, yellow and green food to make the stoplight. (Skittles, melon, peppers) Where do we see stoplights? It is the <u>law</u> to follow stoplights, go, wait, stop!

Story: <u>The Ten Commandments</u>, re-worded by Kim Lyon

1. You should have no other gods before Me.

2. You should not make idols.

3. You should not take the name of the Lord in vain.

4. Remember the Sabbath, and keep it holy.

5. Honor your father and mother.

6. You should never hurt anyone.

7. You should be faithful to your husband or wife.

8. You should not take things that aren't yours.

9. You should always tell the truth.

10. Be happy with what you have. Do not want what others have.

Fine Motor Activity: Make a <u>Ten Commandments</u> Banner to keep at home and begin to learn God's <u>laws</u> from memory.

Large Motor: <u>Red Light, Green Light</u> is a game played throughout the ages. When the children hear 'green light', they walk forward toward the person who is 'it'. When the words 'red light' are given, the children must stop. The winner is the one who gets to the person who is 'it' first and becomes 'it.' Make the association for the children that everyone follows the '<u>law</u>' of the stoplight while walking or driving.

Close in Prayer: Thank You, Father for writing your rules for us. Thank You Father for being the truth, the way, and the life! Amen

Guidance for Parents: <u>Law</u>

Scripture: 1 John 2:1-2, *My little children, I am writing <u>these things</u> to you...*

1 Peter 1:24, *But the <u>word</u> of the LORD endures forever*

Ways to Teach <u>Law</u>: The Ten <u>Commandments</u> give parents the tools needed to teach children morals, values and <u>laws</u>. The Ten <u>Commandments</u> give us a guideline emphasized by God Himself, for the <u>laws</u> of living our lives today. The Ten <u>Commandments</u> are a tool for us to learn who God is. Jesus taught from the Ten <u>Commandments</u>. The book of Proverbs is a guide for parents to have the wisdom to teach their children the Ten <u>Commandments</u>. God is His word. He gives His word in the Bible. He stands on His word. His way is made straight. God does not change. His word stands true and firm throughout the ages. His word does not change with the times, it was written once, and has not been changed.

Songs used today: <u>The B I B L E</u>, Wonder Kids, *30 Bible Songs and 30 Bible Stories*

<u>This is My Commandment</u>, Wonder Kids, *30 Bible Songs and 30 Bible Stories*

Vocabulary Builder: <u>law, word, scripture, commandments</u>

Bible Usage: The word <u>law</u> is used 599 times in the Bible.

- *It is by no means the author's intent to take God's <u>Commandments</u> and rewrite them for any reason other than to reach and teach young children for God's glory! Young children need to grow up learning the <u>Ten Commandments</u>. The vocabulary changes are to reach children by being stated on their reading, listening and comprehending levels. Parents, have a written copy of the <u>Ten Commandments</u> in your home, so children will grow to learn the actual wording given to us by God.*

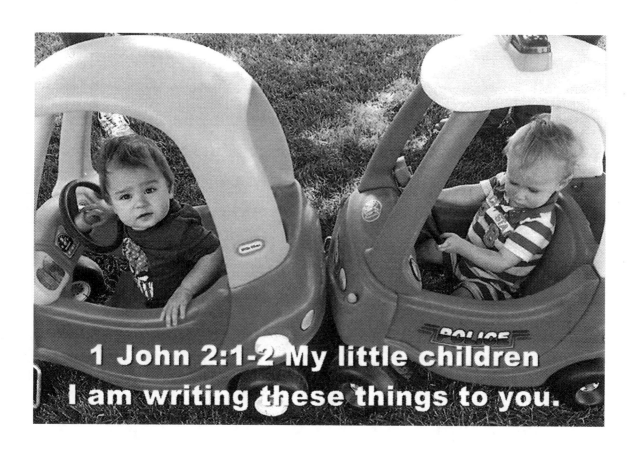

1 John 2:1-2 My little children I am writing these things to you.

The Ten Commandments

1. There is only one God.

2. Nothing is more important than God.

3. Do not take the LORD's name in vain.

4. Sunday is God's special day.

5. Honor your father and mother

6. Do not hurt anyone.

7. Be faithful to your husband or wife.

8. Do not take things that are not yours.

9. Always tell the truth.

10. Do not want what others have.

Lesson 18

Opening Prayer: Dear Father God, We pray today that You will teach us how to put on the armor of God to resist <u>temptation</u>. Thank You for being our strength! Amen

Scripture: Ephesians 6:10-17, *Put on the whole armor of God, that you may be able to stand against the <u>wiles of the devil.</u>*

Vocabulary: <u>temptation</u>

Songs: <u>Trouble is Afoot, Temptation</u>, Veggie Tales, *Larry Boy, The Soundtrack* <u>Dem Bones Gonna Rise Again</u>, The Wonder Kids, *30 Bible Songs and 30 Bible Stories*

Snack: Armor of God: pear half body, red licorice for arms and legs, white cheese stick for sword, Pringle potato chip for shield, face and helmet is a tortilla chip for dipping, hands and feet are slices of mandarin oranges

Story: <u>My Bucket of Temptation,</u> After Easter, Shane had a sand bucket full of candy. His mom put all his candy in the candy bucket. There were M&M's, Skittles, Starburst, and chocolate candy bars in his bucket. Shane's mom let him have ONE piece of candy a day, but that candy was so good, it made Shane's mouth water just to think about it. Every time Shane walked by that yellow candy bucket, he wanted a piece of candy. He asked his mom if he could have some candy. He asked his grandma if he could have some candy. He asked his daddy if he could have some candy. He asked his grandad if he could have some candy. But everyone said, "No." Shane knew he could reach the candy bucket. One day the <u>temptation</u> was too much. Shane knew his mom had already given him his one candy for the day, but when Grandma left the room, Shane walked over to the yellow candy bucket and sat it on the ground. Shane sat down on the ground beside the bucket and started eating candy. As soon as Grandma came into the room, she saw that Shane was eating candy. Shane felt really sorry for making this choice. He knew it was wrong. This is called <u>temptation</u>. That candy bucket was too much to say 'no' to because the <u>temptation</u> was so big. When we have to make a good choice, but <u>temptation</u> gets in our way, we need to pray! God can give us the strength we need to say 'no' to <u>temptation</u>. We can put on the armor of God to be strong!

Fine Motor: Armor of God: Have children literally put on the armor of God. When we are covered in His armor, we are fully protected from evil. We are kept safe! (Armor: Dollar Tree had shields, swords and arm plates; make armor out of brown paper grocery sacks or chest plate, paper plate for shield, and a strip of cardboard for sword.

Large Motor: Wearing God's Armor: role play being dressed in armor. Take photos of the children wearing their armor. What does each piece do to protect us?

Activity: Use project provided for coloring page or paper doll

Salvation (helmet), Truth (shield), Righteousness (breast plate), Peace and Gospel (boots), and the Word of God (sword).

Close in Prayer: Father God, You are love. You love us. You forgive us when we make mistakes. You are strong, when we are <u>tempted</u>. Thank You, Father, for giving us your Son, Jesus. Amen

Parent Guidance: **Temptation**

Scripture: Ephesians 6:10-17 *Put on the whole armor of God, that you may be able to stand against the <u>wiles of the devil.</u>*

Ways to Teach <u>Temptation</u>: <u>Temptation</u> is calling you to sin, but it is not a sin to be <u>tempted</u>. Jesus was <u>tempted</u>, but Jesus is the only person in the history of the world not to sin. Jesus is the only perfect person. We are sinners, and we have to have God's help to make good choices and not to choose sin. Encourage your children to be able to talk openly about <u>temptation</u> in order to keep the doors open for later years when children will battle <u>temptation</u> more often and on more serious issues. It will be important for parents not to become the judge in these situations, or children will learn to avoid these conversations. God is the judge, leave that to Him!

Songs Used Today:

<u>Dem Bones Gonna Rise Again</u>, The Wonder Kids, *30 Bible Songs and 30 Bible Stories*

Vocabulary Builder: <u>temptation, wiles of the devil, choices, tempted</u>

Bible Usage: <u>Temptation</u> is found 23 times in the Bible.

Ephesians 6:13-17
Therefore put on the
full armor of God...

Use with Tasty Armor of God in Lesson 18 - <u>Temptation</u>

Belt of Truth

Sword of the Spirit

Breastplate of Righteousness

Shoes of the Gospel of Truth

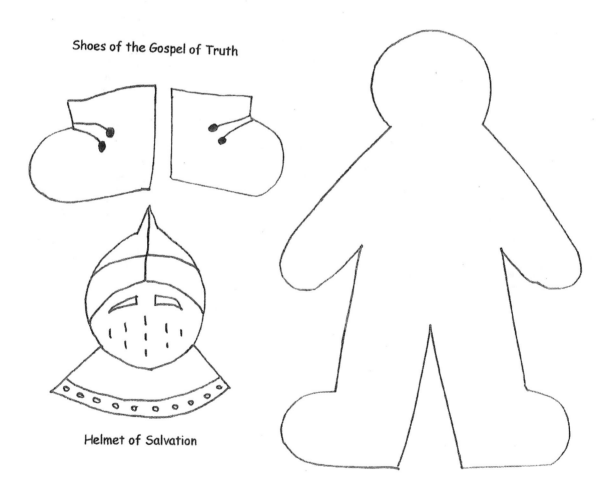

Helmet of Salvation

Ephesians 6:10-17 Put on the whole armor of God...

Lesson 19

Opening Prayer: Thank You Father God for forgiving our <u>sins</u>. Help us learn to be strong enough to say no to <u>sinful</u> choices. Amen

Scripture: James 4:7, *Submit to God. Resist the devil and he will flee from you*

Vocabulary: <u>sin, darkness</u>

Songs: <u>Let Your Light Shine</u>, Hillsong Kids, *Ultimate Collection, (Live)*
<u>This Little Light of Mine</u>, The Wonder Kids, *30 Bible Songs and 30 Bible Stories*

Snack: Safe Driver Snacks: Twinkies, Teddy Grahams, large marshmallows, pretzel (not stick). Cut the large marshmallows in thirds, and each piece will become a wheel. Use the pretzel twist as the steering wheel. The bear is the driver. See photo.

Story: <u>The Street is Not Safe</u>, Eli was busy playing outside in his front yard. He liked to play ball. He threw the ball and chased it. He kicked the ball and chased it. He bounced the ball and chased it. He rolled the ball and chased it. His mom was outside watching him play ball. Sometimes the ball would go close to the street. Mom would say, "Eli, stay out of the street." Eli would stay out of the street and his mom would go get the ball for him. One day, Eli was in the front yard playing ball, and the wind blew the ball into the street! Right away, Eli ran into the street to get the ball! Eli could hear his mom yelling for him to stay out of the street, but Eli was in the street. He stopped and looked and he saw his ball in the street. He saw his mom running toward him. He also saw a car coming very fast toward him and his ball! Eli chose to back up out of the street as fast as he could to get away from the fast car. Eli's mom grabbed him into her arms and gave him a big hug. She thanked him for coming back into the yard, and getting out of the street. The car went by, and mom got the ball for Eli. If Eli would have gone into the street to get the ball, the car might have hurt Eli. If Eli would have gone into the street to get the ball, he would have not obeyed Mom's words about staying out of the street. We <u>sin</u> when we do not follow our rules. We must be careful to follow the rules given to us from our moms and dads. We must be careful to follow the rules given to us from God. He will help us choose not to <u>sin</u>, if we take time to talk to Him about our problems or choices, like going into the street. God will help us make the right choices every day! He will also help us clean up the <u>sin</u>, if we forget to wait on Him. He loves us so much!

Fine Motor: Black Heart: Provide a 4 by 6 inch paper for each child to color. Color the entire paper with pretty colors. Color over it with a black crayon, firmly and solidly. Using a coin, scratch off the black crayon in the shape of a heart. Talk to the children about the beautiful colors as being our heart. The black is <u>sin</u>. <u>Sin</u> is dark. It covers our heart. The coin is God, and only God can clean up our <u>sin</u> as we ask for forgiveness. Use the coin to scrape black off in the shape of a heart. Clean up the heart.

Activity: Let Your Light Shine: Give each child a small battery operated candle, a vegetable can, and a vegetable can with holes punched in it. Talk about the darkness, where the candle is underneath the can. Talk about the light, God, when the candle is out from under any darkness. Talk about the candle underneath the can with holes in it. This is us as we take our 'sin' to God to ask forgiveness, and the darkness comes to light!

Large Motor: This Little Light of Mine: Sing songs again while dancing joyously with the lights!

Close in Prayer: Prayer of repentance. Model how to ask for forgiveness. Model how to bring a <u>sin</u> before the LORD.

Guidance for Parents: **<u>Sin</u>**

Scripture: James 4:7, *Submit to God. Resist the devil, <u>(Sin)</u> and he will flee from you*

Ways to Teach About <u>Sin</u>:

Model: praying, asking, waiting and choosing the right choice.

Play charades acting out what choice would be right in any given situation.

Example: Walking into the street or waiting for mommie to go into the street, eating candy when mommie said not to or waiting until she says it's alright, jumping on the couch or sitting on the couch

<u>Teachable Moment:</u>

God sent His son Jesus to die for our <u>sins.</u> (But Jesus is ALIVE!)

Because of Jesus, we are able to take our problems right to God.

Everyone <u>sins</u>, but it is our job to do our best.

God helps us choose not to <u>sin</u>, if we learn to 'wait' on Him! This means we ask Him what He would want us to do. If we wait and listen, He will guide us to make good choices.

Songs used today:

<u>Let Your Light Shine</u>, Hillsong Kids, *Ultimate Collection, (Live)*

<u>This Little Light of Mine</u>, The Wonder Kids, *30 Bible Songs and 30 Bible Stories*

Vocabulary Builder: <u>sin,</u> darkness, light

Bible Usage: The word <u>sin</u> is used in the Bible 441 times.

90

James 4:7 Submit to God.

Use with Safe Driver Snacks in Lesson 19 – <u>Sin</u>

Use with Black Heart in Lesson 19 - <u>Sin</u>

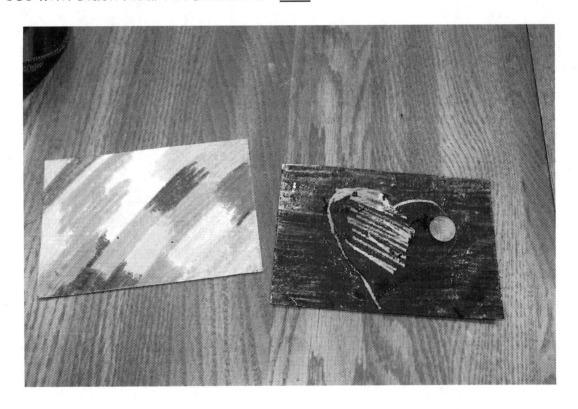

Lesson 20

Opening Prayer: Dear Father God, Thank You for being the one true judge. Thank You for being fair and just. Thank you for teaching us not to judge others.

Scripture: 2 Corinthians 5:10, *For we must all appear at the judgement seat of Christ*

Vocabulary: judgement

Songs: I Will Sing of Mercy and Judgement, Bible Truth Kids, *Bible Songs for Kids*
This is My Commandment, Wonder Kids Sing, *30 Bible Songs and 30 Bible Stories*

Snack: Tea Party: serve cupcakes and ice tea in tea party serving ware, practice best manners!

Story: Being the Judge, Kali and Jillyan were playing house. Kali was the little girl and Jillyan was the mommie. Kali was telling her mommie all about school today. "Amy was mean at recess. Scott has ugly clothes. Jan has short hair that looks like a boy." Jillyan became the mommie right away and said, "You sound like the judge!" Kali asked her pretend mommie, "What's a judge?" Jillyan said a judge is one who decides if people do right or wrong. You are not the judge, and you should not judge other people by the way they look, dress, or act. There is one true judge. Can you guess who that is?" Kali thought for a long time. Finally, Kali said, "I think God is the one true judge." Kali was right. God will decide if people make bad choices, not us. We must be careful not to judge others.

Fine Motor: Lacing Shoes: practice lacing or tying shoes or lace up toys. 'Judge' the progress.

Large Motor: Someone Else's Shoes: People say, "Don't judge someone until you've walked in their shoes." Have a few pairs of shoes to look at. What judgements can we make about people by looking at their shoes? Do we know for sure? No. We would have to ask the person who wears these shoes. (Parents in to verify our guesses. Ex: Baseball Shoes, Do you play baseball? Fireman's Boots, Do you put out fires? Clean Baby Shoes, Do you walk yet? Ballet Shoes, Do you like to dance?)

Activity: Judging Others: look at photos of different people. Ask if they are good people or bad people. How do you know? If you had an answer, you are looking at someone and making judgements. It is easy to make judgements, but we are asked not to by God. God is the judge!

Close in Prayer: Dear Father, Thank You for being the one true Judge. Please help me not to form judgements about others. Please forgive me for making judgements about other people as I learn. Amen

Guidance for Parents: # Judgement

Scripture: 2 Corinthians 5:10, *For we must all appear at the <u>judgement</u> seat of Christ*

Teaching <u>Judgement</u>:

Jellybean <u>Judgements</u>: Give your child 10 jellybeans for the day. Each time you catch your child talking about someone in a <u>judgemental</u> way, they give up one jellybean. At the end of the day, the jellybeans that were kept by the child can be eaten!

<u>Judgemental</u> T.V.: If your child is understanding <u>judgements</u>, (talking about people), turn on a t.v. news show. Listen for <u>judgements</u> and point it out to your child. Discuss.

The goal is to learn that God is the <u>judge</u>, and we are not to <u>judge</u> others.

Songs used today: <u>I Will Sing of Mercy and Judgement</u>, Bible Truth Kids, *Bible Songs for Kids*

<u>This is My Commandment</u>, Wonder Kids Sing, *30 Bible Songs and 30 Bible Stories*

Vocabulary Builder: <u>judgement</u>

Bible Usage: The word <u>judgement</u> is used in the Bible 344 times.

2 Corinthians 5:10
For we must all appear at the
judgement seat of Christ.

Generations, Iniquity

Lesson 21

Opening Prayer: Dear Father God, Thank You for my daddy, my grandpa and my great grandpa. Thank You for the <u>generations</u> of my family. Please forgive me any <u>iniquities</u> in my family line. Amen

Scripture: Psalms 112:2, *The <u>generation</u> of the upright will be blessed.*

Vocabulary: <u>generations, iniquity</u>

Songs: <u>Next Generation</u>, Tallowood Kids, *The Doorpost Songs: Next Generation*

<u>The Grandparents' Song</u>, Shana Banana, *Song in My Pocket*

<u>We Are Climbing Jacob's Ladder</u>, The Wonder Kids, *30 Bible Songs and 30 Bible Stories*

Snack: Jello Jigglers: My grandma always made Jello Jigglers for our snack.

Story: <u>The Fourth of July</u>, On the Fourth of July, my family gets together to shoot fireworks. When our family gets together, we have four <u>generations</u>. First, there's me, then my mom, then my mom's daddy, then my grandad's daddy. That's a lot of family! When we are all together we tell stories about our family. I hear mom tell stories about her little girl days. My great grandpa has been in the family longer than all of us. He remembers all of us as babies, and watched us grow bigger. He can tell us stories about days long ago. He likes to say prayers for our family. He knows our family

<u>iniquities</u> that must be broken and forgiven. He knows what we need to pray for to be closer to God. We all want to be close to God!

Fine Motor: Games Through the <u>Generations</u>: Play old fashioned games played by previous <u>generations</u> like Jacks or Jacob's Ladder.

Large Motor: Games Through the <u>Generations</u>: Play old fashioned games played by previous <u>generations.</u> Hopscotch, Red Light, Green Light or Mother May I?

Activity: Family Love Song: Silly movement song to the tune of <u>Happy All the Time</u>… My grandma's, grandma's, grandma's grandma loved me all the time. My grandma's, grandma's, grandma's, grandma loved me all the time. Since Jesus Christ came in, and cleansed my heart of sin, My grandma's, grandma's, grandma's, grandma loved me all the time.

Verse 2: My grandpa's, grandpa's, grandpa's, grandpa loved me all the time. My grandpa's, grandpa's, grandpa's, grandpa loved me all the time. Since Jesus Christ came in, and cleansed my heart of sin, My grandpa's, grandpa's, grandpa's, grandpa loved me all the time.

Verse 3: My mommie's…   Verse 4: My daddy's….

Close in Prayer: Thank You, God for being my Heavenly Father. Thank You for giving me an Earthly father, too! Thank You for giving me the family I love. Amen

Generations

Scripture: Psalms 112:2, *The <u>generation</u> of the upright will be blessed.*

Ways to Break <u>Iniquity</u> in Your Family: If a known sin is prevalent throughout the <u>generations</u> of your family, it needs to be broken off your family line for your children's sake. Be sure you have taken known sins before God and asked for forgiveness. While in an attitude of prayer, bring the sin before God, and ask that it be broken off your family line (future <u>generations</u>), your children and yourself. Declare it to be covered by Jesus' blood. Declare it to never return to your family. Lay the iniquity before God and ask for forgiveness for your family, previous <u>generations</u> or yourself. Be thankful for God's love and forgiveness. Be thankful for His Son, Jesus Christ, and declare this prayer to be in His Son's name. Be sure to fill that empty void with the love of Jesus. Amen

*Jesus was sent to Earth by God to die for our sins (although He rose again!), and we can claim that to rid ourselves of <u>iniquities.</u>

*While praying prayers like this, use a firm voice and forceful attitude.

Teachable Moment:

Mommie's mommie is grandma.
Daddy's mommie is grandma.
Great grandparents?

Mommie's daddy is grandpa.
Daddy's daddy is grandpa.
Aunts, uncles and cousins are brothers and sisters.

Pray for grandparents.
Pray for your future grandchildren.

Pray for your future children.
Pray for your children's future spouses.

Songs: <u>The Grandparents' Song</u>, Shana Banana, *Song in My Pocket*

<u>We Are Climbing Jacob's Ladder</u>, The Wonder Kids, *30 Bible Songs and 30 Bible Stories*

Vocabulary Builder: <u>generations, iniquity</u>

Bible Usage: The word <u>iniquity</u> is used in the Bible 289 times.

Psalm 112:2
The generations of the
upright will be blessed.

Healed

Lesson 22

Opening Prayer: Dear Jesus, Thank You for taking our (owies, hurts, bruises, illnesses, diseases, burdens, iniquities) and making us well and whole! You died for us, so we can live! Thank you, Jesus. Amen

Scripture: Isaiah 53:5, *By His stripes, we are <u>healed.</u>*

Vocabulary: <u>healed</u>

Songs: <u>Dem Bones Gonna Rise Again</u>, The Wonder Kids, *30 Bible Songs and 30 Bible Stories*

<u>Jesus Loves Even Me</u>, The Wonder Kids, *30 Bible Songs and 30 Bible Stories*

Snack: Get Well Mix: use any ingredients to mix together for snack. Teddy Grahams, marshmallows, chocolate chips, cheese crackers, sunflower seeds, etc.

Story: <u>Jesus Heals</u>, by Kim Lyon, Shane was learning to ride his bike. He rode it up hills and down hills. He rode it up the sidewalk and down the sidewalk. He rode it fast and he rode it slow. He rode it faster and faster. Shane was riding so fast, he went down the hill and off the sidewalk. The bike tipped off the sidewalk and Shane crashed to the ground. When Shane crashed to the ground, he skinned his knee. Shane cried because the bike crash scared him. He cried because his scraped knee was bleeding. Mom came running to help <u>Shane</u>. She saw his knee was scraped and gave it a kiss. When mom got the scrape cleaned up, she put ointment on his knee. She told Shane that Jesus helps <u>heal</u> people's scrapes and scratches. Jesus helps <u>heal</u> people's illnesses and diseases. So mom put on the ointment and told Shane to have faith that Jesus would <u>heal</u> his scraped knee. Then Shane helped mom put a Bandaid on the knee. It already felt better! Shane knew he could pray to Jesus for <u>healing</u>!

Activity: <u>Healing</u> Hearts: each child has a large heart, Bandaids and pretend ointment to apply like we apply faith as we pray to Jesus for healing.

Large Motor: Hopscotch Hearts: draw a hopscotch board on the sidewalk or cut red hearts to play indoors. Practice one foot, two feet pattern of hopping.

Close in Prayer: Thank You, Father for sending your Son Jesus to us for our <u>healing</u>. Jesus bore our scrapes, bruises, owies, illnesses, diseases and other problems with our bodies. We can pray to Jesus for <u>healing</u> and apply faith because we know the truth in your word. Isaiah 53:5, *By His stripes, we are <u>healed</u>*. Amen

Guidance for Parents: **Healed**

Scripture: Isaiah 53:5, *By His stripes, we are <u>healed.</u>*

Ways to Teach <u>Healing</u>: When Jesus was beaten and whipped, He was taking all of the 'yuck' we have in our lives caused by sin. He took the beating and whipping so we don't have to. He took all of our diseases and illnesses. He took all of our aches, pains and unhappiness. All we have to do is learn how to hand those illnesses, diseases and pains back to Him. We have to learn to pray the scripture: Isaiah 53:5, *By His stripes, we are <u>healed.</u>* We pray this scripture and stand in faith for our physical <u>healing.</u> It IS possible and Jesus wants us to live a life free of the 'yuck', so we can fulfill the purpose God created us for! This is exciting news for living in God's Kingdom!

Teachable Moment: Mark 6:2

Jesus <u>heals</u> people in the Bible. Find places in the Bible that tell stories of Jesus <u>healing</u> people. (Matthew, Mark, Luke and John)

Teach your child to pray for <u>healing</u> when they have a health issue. New tooth pain, stuffy nose, scraped knee, etc. Teach them to pray and stand in faith to wait on Jesus to do the <u>healing.</u> Believe!

Songs used today: <u>Dem Bones Gonna Rise Again</u>, The Wonder Kids, *30 Bible Songs and 30 Bible Stories*

<u>Jesus Loves Even Me</u>, The Wonder Kids, *30 Bible Songs and 30 Bible Stories*

Vocabulary Builder: <u>healed</u>

Bible Usage: The word <u>healed</u> is used in the Bible 79 times.

<u>Healing</u> 14, <u>Heal</u> 40, <u>Healeth</u> 4, and <u>Healer</u> 1 = 138

Isaiah 53:5
By His stripes,
we are healed.

Lesson 23

Opening Prayer: Dear Jesus, Thank You for teaching us by your example, how to choose the right choices. We want to be <u>righteous</u>! Amen

Scripture: Matthew 6:33, *But seek ye first the kingdom of God, and His <u>righteousness,</u> and all these things shall be added unto you.* 1 John 3:7, *Little children, let no one deceive you. Whoever practices <u>righteousness</u> is <u>righteous</u>, as He is <u>righteous.</u>*

Vocabulary: <u>righteous, righteousness</u>

Songs: <u>Life, Righteousness and Honor</u>, Bible Truth Music, *Bible Songs for Kids, #7*

Snack: Breastplate of <u>Righteousness</u>: Use a hot dog for each child. Cut top half in three pieces, which will be head, and two arms. Cut bottom half in two pieces, which will be the legs. Microwave each snack up to one minute. Cut a <u>righteousness</u> breastplate from a slice of cheese and lay on top of the hot dog. See photo.

Story: <u>Right and Wrong</u>, Justin was learning to color and draw pictures. Justin's mom bought him markers. Justin liked to use the markers on his paper. Justin liked using the markers to color and draw. Justin colored his paper until it was full. Then Justin colored his arms and legs. Justin still wanted to color, so he thought about it, and then made the choice to color on the wall. Justin colored and colored with his marker on the wall. Then Justin started to feel bad. He stopped coloring and looked at the wall. Justin knew he had made a mistake. Justin knew he had made the wrong choice. He went to his mom and showed her what he had done to the wall. Mom told him that he had not made the <u>right</u> choice. Coloring on paper is the <u>right</u> choice. Coloring on the wall is the wrong choice. Justin's mom helped him clean the coloring off the wall. Now the wall looks as good as new! If we make a wrong choice, it is important that we go to God and have Him help us clean it up! When we choose <u>right</u>, we are <u>righteous</u>.

Fine Motor: <u>Righteousness</u> Breastplate: Use Playdough to make a copy of today's snack. Roll out a head, body, arms and legs. Form a breastplate from a second color.

Large Motor: Full Armor of God: play charades as all kids don themselves with the full armor of God. Put on the breastplate of <u>Righteousness</u>, helmet of Salvation, sword of the Spirit, belt of Truth, shield of Faith, and shoes of the gospel of Peace.

Activity: The Breastplate of <u>Righteousness</u>: use the breastplate of <u>Righteousness</u> (a paper plate) as a 'paddle' with a balloon. Throw the balloon (sin) into the air and use the plate as a breastplate that keeps the balloon away from us.

Close in Prayer: Dear God, Thank You for always being there for us as we learn how to discern <u>right</u> from wrong. We want to be really good at practicing <u>righteousness</u>! Amen

Guidance for Parents: # Righteousness

Scripture: Matthew 6:33, *But seek ye first the kingdom of God, and His* <u>*righteousness*</u>*, and all these things shall be added unto you.* 1 John 3:7, *Little children, let no one deceive you. Whoever practices* <u>*righteousness*</u> *is* <u>*righteous*</u>*, as He is* <u>*righteous.*</u>

<u>Teachable Moment:</u>

Beginning with Adam and Eve in the Garden with the Tree of Life, God has given each of us the freedom to make choices. Because Eve chose to eat from the apple, Satan gained the right to rule and reign in an evil realm on Earth. He is in constant competition with Almighty God for control of our lives. Children can be taught and encouraged to make the <u>right</u> choices at an early age. This struggle and choice will last throughout our lifetimes. There is a heaven and a hell. Teach your child to be discerning. What feels right? What do you think Jesus would do? Continue to teach your child to pray to God for answers and guidance. Teach your child to wait on the Lord for answers before acting. Making the <u>right</u> choice is practicing <u>righteousness</u>. A person who practices <u>righteousness</u> is <u>righteous</u>.

Songs used today:

<u>Life, Righteousness and Honor</u>, Bible Truth Music, *Bible Songs for Kids, #7*

Vocabulary Builder: <u>righteousness, righteous</u>

Bible Usage: The word <u>righteousness</u> is found 322 times in the Bible, and <u>righteous</u> is found 284 times.

Matthew 6:33
But seek ye first the
kingdom of God,
and his righteousness.

Lesson 24

Opening Prayer: Dear Father, Thank You for your <u>grace</u>. Your <u>grace</u> shows us how much You love us! Sometimes we make wrong choices, but You still show us <u>grace</u>. Thank You for your loving <u>grace</u>. Amen

Scripture: Ephesians 2:8-9, *unmerited love and favor of God toward men*

Vocabulary: <u>grace</u>

Songs: <u>Amazing Grace, My Chains are Gone</u>, Michael W. Smith, *A New Hallelujah*

<u>My God is So Big,</u> Various Artists, *25 Bible Action Songs*

Snack: God's <u>Grace</u> Trail Mix: pretzels for forgiveness, red M&M's for love, rice cereal for our creation, corn cereal for provision, mini marshmallows for healing, bread bites for covering all our needs (Chex Mix)

Story: <u>Amazing Grace</u>, by Kim Lyon, Amazing <u>Grace</u> is the love we get every day from God. Amazing <u>Grace</u> is a song we sing at Church. Amazing <u>Grace</u> is also a person! Amazing <u>Grace</u> is a little girl. She is seven years old. She loves her mom. She loves her daddy. She loves her brothers and sisters. Amazing <u>Grace</u> is amazing, because of how much she loves God. She loves God in the morning when she wakes up. She loves God in the daytime, when she works at school, or plays at home. She loves God at nighttime while she gets ready to go to bed to get the sleep she needs. Amazing <u>Grace</u> talks to God about things that make her sad. She talks to God about things that make her happy. She talks to God about things she knows people need. She talks to God about how good God is to her. She talks to God about what He wants her to do each and every day. Amazing <u>Grace</u> loves God. God loves Amazing <u>Grace</u>! <u>Grace</u> from God is an amazing forgiveness of sins. God's <u>grace</u> is a love so wonderful, we can't imagine how big and good it is. God's <u>grace</u> is a love so perfect, we can't earn it, or work for it, or deserve it. God's <u>grace</u> is a love so gigantic if it could be measured by size, we can't take it all in and understand how wonderful it is. Make sure you ask for forgiveness of your sins. Make sure you talk to God every day about His Amazing <u>Grace</u>!

Large Motor: <u>Graceful</u> Dancing: use scarves for dancing to <u>Amazing Grace</u>

Fine Motor Activity: Amazing <u>Grace</u>: preparation needed ahead of time: use glue to draw a large heart and the word <u>grace</u> on a large piece of paper for each child. When it dries, it will be nearly invisible. Give each child the piece of paper with the invisible message on it and water colors. As the kids paint, the picture appears! God's <u>grace</u> is not seen, but it is all around us in an amazing way.

Close in Prayer: Thank you, Father for your <u>grace</u>! You are an amazing Father. Thank You for loving us. Amen

Guidance for Parents: # Grace

Scripture: Ephesians 2:8-9, ... *unmerited love and favor of God toward men*

Ways to Define <u>Grace</u>:

He forgives us	He loves us unconditionally
He created us	He provides for us
He teaches us	He heals us

He is so big, He covers us with Himself for all purposes. But He gives us the choice to choose Him.

*Find a small doll or item and put it on the floor. Use a really large blanket to cover this small item. Help your child understand that the small item is the child, and the blanket is God's <u>grace</u>. He covers us with everything we need.

*Only by <u>grace</u> can we receive God and His goodness, His forgiveness, His love, access to His power, His Son and His gifts.

*Only by accepting Jesus Christ, His son, can we receive <u>grace</u>.

*Sometimes we misconceive the easiness of asking for forgiveness. Sometimes we do the misdeed while fully aware of choosing to sin. It is easy to fall in the trap of believing that while God's <u>grace</u> and forgiveness is given so easily, it's ok to sin and just ask for forgiveness. NO! We need to learn the reverence, the fear of the Lord. He is so great, we need to revere His presence in our lives and not take Him for granted. We need to follow the rules He carefully laid out for our lives by 'doing the work' He asks us to do. He is full of joy when we make the well thought out choice to obey His rules and to love Him.

Songs used today: <u>Amazing Grace, My Chains are Gone</u>, Michael W. Smith, *A New Hallelujah*
<u>My God is So Big</u>, Various Artists, *25 Bible Action Songs*

Vocabulary Builder: <u>grace</u>

Bible Usage: The word <u>grace</u> is used in the Bible 206 times.

Ephesians 2:8-9
...unmerited love and
favor of God...

Use with Amazing Grace in Lesson 24 - <u>Grace</u>

Paint the word <u>Grace</u> with glue in different ways on large pieces of paper so each child has
one, and allow to dry overnight. This will be done prior to lesson day. Using watercolors,
paint over the top and watch <u>grace</u> 'appear.'

Lesson 25

Opening Prayer: Thank You Father God that we are <u>blessed</u> to be together today to learn more about You. Amen

Scripture: 2 Corinthians 9:8, *And God is able to <u>bless</u> you abundantly...(so that in all things at all times, having all that you need, you will abound in every good work.)*

Vocabulary: <u>bless, blessed</u>

Songs: <u>Blessed Be the Lord</u>, Various Artists, 51 *Must Have Worship Songs for Kids*

Snack: Bountiful Butterflies: fill a snack sized baggie with two snacks such as grapes and Fruit Loops. Put the grapes on one side and the Fruit Loops on the other. Gather the bag together and place a clothespin in the center. Add eyes, antennas, and brown crayon, marker, or paint as desired to look like a butterfly. See photo.

Story: <u>I Am Blessed!</u> "I am so <u>blessed</u>", Shane heard his dad say every day. "We are so <u>blessed</u>", Shane heard his mom say every day. What does it mean? Shane wondered. "We are <u>blessed</u> to have our house to stay in while it is storming," said Dad. "We are <u>blessed</u> to have food on our table every day," said Mom. Shane asked his mom, "Why are we <u>blessed</u> to have food on our table every day?" "We are <u>blessed</u> because some people don't have food tonight and we always do. There are kids with hungry tummies," answered Mom. "Yes, and some kids don't have a house to live in when it is storming. They are homeless," said Dad. "Shane, how has God <u>blessed</u> you?" asked Dad. Shane thought and thought. He smiled and ran into his room. He came back with animals. He ran into his room again and came out with more animals. He ran at top speed into his bedroom one more time and came out with a basket of animals. He went to the couch, pulled off the cushions, and started setting his animals on the couch. When he was finished, he was so excited! He had made a zoo! "I am <u>blessed</u> with many animals!" Shane told his mom and dad. God places so many <u>blessings</u> on us each and every day. We need to thank God for His endless <u>blessings</u> each and every day.

Fine Motor Activity: Butterfly <u>Blessings</u>: Loosely gather colorful tissue paper and place it in the mouth of a clothespin. Add brown crayon, antennas and eyes as desired. See photo.

Large Motor: Soaring Butterflies: Sing fun made up songs about butterflies while waving scarves in the air as butterfly wings. Song 1: to the tune of <u>Ten Little Indians</u>, One little, two little, three little butterflies, four little, five little, six little butterflies, seven little, eight little, nine little butterflies, ten little butterflies soaring through the air. Song 2: to the tune of <u>How Much is That Doggie in the Window</u>, How much is that butterfly in the window? The one with the beautiful wings. How much is that butterfly in the window? I do hope that butterfly's for sale. Cuz I want that butterfly in the window. The one with the beautiful wings. Cuz I want that butterfly in the window. I do hope that butterfly's for sale.

Close in Prayer: Dear Father God, You are such a <u>blessing</u> in my life! You make life amazing! Thank You for <u>blessing</u> me with my family, friends, my home and my Church! Amen

Guidance for Parents: **Blessed**

Scripture: 2 Corinthians 9:8, *And God is able to <u>bless</u> you abundantly...so that in all things at all times, having all that you need, you will abound in every good work.*

Ways to Teach <u>Blessings</u>:

How does God <u>bless</u> us?

How do we <u>bless</u> others?

Make a list or a booklet of <u>blessings</u> in your life.

Talk about children who live in poverty. Not everyone is as <u>blessed</u> as we are!

Songs used today:

<u>Blessed Be the Lord</u>, Various Artists, 51 *Must Have Worship Songs for Kids*

Vocabulary Builder: <u>bless, blessed</u>

Bible Usage: The word <u>bless</u> is found in the Bible 164, and <u>blessed</u> 345 times.

2 Corinthians 9:8
And God is able to
bless you abundantly...

Use with Bountiful Butterflies in Lesson 25 – <u>Blessed</u>

Use with Butterfly <u>Blessings</u> in Lesson 25 – <u>Blessed</u>

Lesson 26

Opening Prayer: Dear Father God, To You be the glory! You glorify your Son, Jesus glorifies You, and we glorify You and Jesus! Amen

Scripture: John 1:14, *...and we have seen His glory, glory as of the only Son from the Father, full of grace and truth*

Vocabulary: glory

Songs: Living to Glory (Colossians 3:12), Caleb Campbell, *Children's Prayers – Praying the Bible*

Noah's Arky Arky, The Wonder Kids, *30 Bible Songs and 30 Bible Stories*

Snack: Noah's Ark: Build Noah's Ark from making peanut butter sandwiches and cutting the sandwich in half. Round off the bottom corners to be a half circle and call this the ark. Use animal crackers in pairs to bring to the ark. See photo.

Story: Shane and His Daddy, Shane gets to go to work with his daddy. Shane watches his daddy and tries to work just like daddy. If Daddy picks up books, Shane picks up books. If Daddy runs the vacuum, Shane tries to run the vacuum. When Daddy mows the yard, Shane mows the yard. When Daddy works in the garden, Shane works in the garden. Shane loves his daddy so much, he wants to be just like him. Jerome loves his son so much, he loves spending time with his son. Jesus loves His father, and the Father loves His Son. Jesus loves giving His Father all the glory. God loves giving His Son all the glory. When we do things, we should do it for God and His Son's glory. When we work in the garden, we give God the glory for our blessings of land, water, sun and seeds. When we mow the yard, we give God the <u>glory</u> again for the blessings of land, water, sun and equipment we use in our yards. When God asked Noah to build an ark, Noah built the ark for God's <u>glory</u>. When God asked Noah to take care of His animals, Noah took care of God's animals, and he did it for God's <u>glory</u>. When God used His power to stop the flood, He sent a rainbow and a dove. Noah saw God's <u>glory</u>. God sent the rainbow as a promise that He would never flood the entire Earth again. God's <u>glory</u>! God sent the dove, and we think of the Holy Spirit that God sent when we see a dove. God's <u>glory</u>! God's <u>glory</u> is full of grace and truth! We are overwhelmed with God's love and <u>glory</u>.

Fine Motor: Triangle Trinity: using colored craft sticks with Velcro on the ends, form a triangle. On the top, put a crown for God, bottom left, put a heart for Jesus coming to the Earth like one of us, and for the Holy Spirit, put a dove that lives within us. Trinity means three. God, Jesus and the Holy Spirit are the three in one.

Large Motor: Animal Walk: walk like these animals walk, bear, crab, tiger, penguin, fish, snake, kangaroo, monkey, etc.

Activity: Noah's Arky Arky: place two paper plates back to back. Staple the plates around the outside edge. Cut in half to have two arks. Color, cut and place two of each animal inside the ark.

Close in Prayer: Dear Father God, Help us make the choices that <u>glorify</u> You as our wonderful Father in Heaven, and your kingdom right here on Earth! Amen

Guidance for Parents: __Glory__

Scripture: John 1:14, *...and we have seen His _glory_, _glory_ as of the only Son from the Father, full of grace and truth*

Teachable Moment:

The Lord's Prayer, Matthew 6:9-13, continue to learn from memory.

Colossians 3:12

Read a variety of books or Bible stories about Noah's Ark. Compare them with your child. How are they the same? How are they different?

Read other Bible stories. Can you find God's _glory_? His _glory_ is grace and truth.

Songs used today: __Living to Glory (Colossians 3:12)__, Caleb Campbell, *Children's Prayers – Praying the Bible*

__Noah's Arky Arky__, The Wonder Kids, *30 Bible Songs and 30 Bible Stories*

Vocabulary Builder: __Glory__

Bible Usage: The word __glory__ is used in the Bible 480 times.

John 1:14 ...and we have seen His glory...

Use with Noah's Arky Arky in Lesson 26 - <u>Glory</u>

Use with Noah's Ark in Lesson 26 – <u>Glory</u>

Use with <u>Wiseguys</u> in Lesson 27 – <u>Wisdom</u>

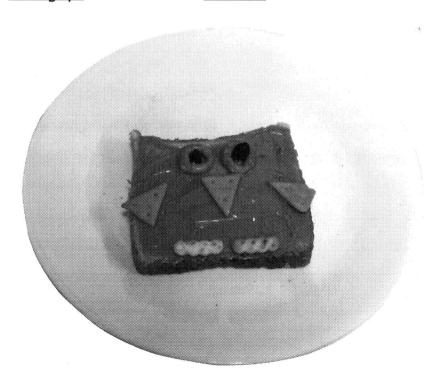

Lesson 27

Opening Prayer: Dear Father, You are so <u>wise</u>! You are so creative in your plans for us. Thank You for giving us the commandments. Help us grow <u>wise</u> by learning your rules. Amen

Scripture: Proverbs 10:8, *The <u>wise</u> in heart will receive commandments*

Vocabulary: <u>wisdom</u>

Songs: <u>This is My Commandment</u>, The Wonder Kids, *30 Bible Songs and 30 Bible Stories*

Snack: <u>Wiseguys</u>: owls made out of bread, cheese and fruit.

Story: <u>Learn God's Word!</u>, Eli asked his mom, "Mommie, how do you know what God's rules are?" Eli's mom told him that was a very good question! "God wrote His rules for us in the Bible," Eli's mom told him. "God calls these rules, <u>The Ten Commandments</u>, and all of God's people need to learn them," Eli's mom explained. Eli and his mom went to find Eli's Bible. Sure enough! God's <u>Ten Commandments</u> were in his Bible. Eli and his mom began to learn the <u>Ten Commandments</u> for kids together.

1. You should have no other gods before Me.

2. You should not make idols.

3. You should not take the name of the Lord in vain.

4. Remember the Sabbath, and keep it holy.

5. Honor your father and mother.

6. You should never hurt anyone.

7. You should be faithful to your husband or wife.

8. You should not take things that aren't yours.

9. You should always tell the truth.

10. Be happy with what you have. Do not want what others have.

Rules are healthy for us. They help us know how to act so we can be like Jesus! When we study and learn God's words from the Bible, we grow in <u>wisdom</u>.

Fine Motor Activity: Make a <u>Ten Commandment</u> Booklet

Large Motor: Question or Command: Play like Simon Says. If it is a command, do what is said. If it is a question, don't move! Example: Jump! is a command. It is a firm statement. Can you jump? is not saying to do it. It is a question, not a command. God gave commandments because He wants them done!

Close in Prayer: Thank You, Father God for giving us your rules. You love us so much, You sent your <u>Ten Commandments</u> to teach us how to love You in return, and how to live in your kingdom. Amen

Guidance for Parents: # Wisdom

Scripture: Proverbs 10:8, *The <u>wise</u> in heart will receive commandments*

Teachable Moment: Learn God's Word! Exodus: 20

Teach your child the <u>Ten Commandments</u>. Use language your child will understand at each age through the years, until they know the commandments as God gave them to Moses.

*Read: <u>The Ten Commandments</u>, by Kim Lyon

*Relate these commandments to experiences in your child's life.

*Review often!

*<u>Wisdom</u> is when we learn and become <u>wise</u>. Learning God's commandments are of top importance in our lives!

Songs used today: <u>This is My Commandment</u>, The Wonder Kids, *30 Bible Songs and 30 Bible Stories*

Vocabulary Builder: <u>wisdom</u>, commandment

Bible Usage: The word <u>wisdom</u> is found in the Bible 345 times.

- *It is by no means the author's intent to take God's Commandments and rewrite them for any reason other than to reach and teach young children for God's glory! Young children need to grow up learning the <u>Ten Commandments</u>. The vocabulary changes are to reach children by being stated on their reading, listening and comprehending levels. Parents should have a written copy of the <u>Ten Commandments</u> at home, so children will grow to learn the actual wording given to us by God.*

**Proverbs 10:8
The wise in heart
will receive commandments**

GOD'S TEN COMMANDMENTS
(Deuteronomy 5:5-21)

I. I, the Lord, am your God, who brought you out of the land of Egypt, that place of slavery. You shall not have other gods besides me.

II. You shall not take the name of the Lord, your God, in vain. For the Lord will not leave unpunished him who takes his name in vain.

III. Take care to keep holy the Sabbath day as the Lord, your God, commanded you. Six days you may labor and do all your work; but the seventh day is the Sabbath of the...

IV. Honor your father and your mother.

V. You shall not kill.

VI. You shall not commit adultery.

VII. You shall not steal.

VIII. You shall not bear dishonest witness against your neighbor.

IX. You shall not covet your neighbor's wife.

X. You shall not desire your neighbor's house or field nor anything that belongs to him.

Use with Make a Ten Commandment Booklet in Lesson 27 – Wisdom

Cut out each commandment and glue on the front of a letter sized envelope.
Cut photos from newspapers or magazines to fit each commandment.

The Ten Commandments

Commandment One:
There is only one God.

Commandment Two:
Nothing is more important
than God.

Commandment Three:
Do not take the Lord's
name in vain.

Commandment Four:

Sunday is God's special day.

Commandment Five:

Honor your father and mother.

Commandment Six:

You should not hurt anyone.

Commandment Seven:

You should be faithful to your

family.

Commandment Eight:

You should not take things

that aren't yours.

Commandment Nine:

You should always tell the truth.

Commandment Ten:

Do not want what others have.

Lesson 28

Opening Prayer: Father God, Thank You for loving us. Thank You for bringing <u>peace</u> to us when we are nervous or afraid. Please be with us as we learn about You! Amen

Scripture: John 14:27, *<u>Peace</u> I leave with you. My <u>peace</u> I give to you; not as the world gives do I give to you. Let not your heart be troubled, neither let it be afraid.*

Vocabulary: <u>peace</u>

Songs: <u>I've Got Peace Like a River</u>, Countdown Kids, *We Worship and Adore* <u>Standing on the Promises,</u> Kidzup Kids, *Worship Together* <u>You are Holy (Prince of Peace),</u> Cedarmont Kids, *Cedarmont Worship for Kids, Vol. 1*

Snack Activity: <u>Peace</u> Pieces, Make a necklace out of edible pieces. Use Fruit Loops, and add a <u>peace</u> sign in the center. Wear and eat!

Story: <u>Bedtime Peace</u>, It was time to go to bed. Bedtime made Ruby cranky. Ruby was cranky because she was unsettled at bedtime. She didn't want to go to bed. She didn't feel like she could relax and go to sleep. Ruby cried out to her mom. When mom came into Ruby's room, she asked Ruby what was wrong. Ruby told her mom, she didn't want to go to bed. Ruby's mom explained to Ruby that she was tired and it was time to rest her body, and sleep for the night. Ruby's mom said that Ruby was safe in her bed with mom and daddy in the next room. Ruby still continued to fuss about going to bed. Ruby's mom asked Ruby if she wanted to pray that she would feel better at bedtime. Ruby said, "Yes." Mom prayed to our most wonderful

Father God and asked Him that Ruby would feel His <u>peace</u>. She asked Him to stay close to Ruby while she slept, and grant her His <u>peace</u>. Mom told Ruby that God takes care of problems like that for us. She told Ruby to snuggle into her bed and to feel like God was holding her ALL night long. She was wrapped and cuddled in God's <u>peace</u> filled presence. Ruby was ready to go to sleep!

Fine Motor: <u>Peace</u> Races: lay narrow, colored paper strips on the table. Give each child a straw and pieces of cereal. (Fruit Loops) Use the straw to blow the cereal from one end of the colored trail to the end, and eat it!

Large Motor: <u>Peaceful</u> Poses: lay colored circles around the room on the floor. Have kids hop with both feet from color to color as you call colors. Limit to four colors or so and provide one of each color for each child. Have the kids pretend to be penguins and the colored circles are icebergs. Hop on and strike a pose! A <u>peaceful</u> pose, because they are safe.

Close in Prayer: Thank You Father God for our time to learn about You. Please teach us to pray to You when we need to feel your <u>peace</u>. Amen

Guidance for Parents: ## Peace

Scripture: John 14:27, _Peace I leave with you. My peace I give to you; not as the world gives do I give to you. Let not your heart be troubled, neither let it be afraid._

Teachable Moment: Romans 5:1-5, Therefore, since we have been justified through faith, we have peace with God through our Lord Jesus Christ, 2 through whom we have gained access by faith into this grace in which we now stand. And we boast in the hope of the glory of God. 3 Not only so, but we also glory in our sufferings, because we know suffering produces perseverance, 4 perseverance, character, and character, hope. 5 And hope does not put us to shame, because God's love has been poured out into our hearts through the Holy Spirit, who has been given to us. (Continue reading 5:6-11)

This has been added as a reminder to each one of us how remarkable the gift of the Trinity is to our very being. It is important that children begin to understand the 'being' of each of the Three in One: God, Jesus and the Holy Spirit. Begin to teach your child how to pray to each of the three. God: the Father, the Creator, the Provider, the LORD, our heavenly Father, pray: thankfulness, praise, worship, honor, requests

Jesus: the Son, our Savior, our King, our Lord, the Prince

Pray: healing, forgiveness, peace, protection,

The Holy Spirit: our constant companion, our inner voice, our spirit, our friend, a witness to us

Pray: guidance, choices, to hear from God, talk about daily living, constant conversation

Read: <u>God, Jesus, and The Holy Spirit</u>, by Kim Lyon

Songs used today:

<u>I've Got Peace Like a River</u>, Countdown Kids, *We Worship and Adore*
<u>Standing on the Promises,</u> Kidzup Kids, *Worship Together*
<u>You are Holy (Prince of Peace),</u> Cedarmont Kids, *Cedarmont Worship for Kids, Vol. 1*

Vocabulary Builder: <u>peace</u>

Bible Usage: The word <u>peace</u> is used in the Bible 470 times.

John 14:27 ...My peace I give to you...

Lesson 29

Opening Prayer: Dear Father God, 'Your <u>mercy</u> endures forever', means You love us so much! Thank You for your love, your forgiveness and your generous blessings! Amen

Scripture: Psalm 136:3, *"give thanks to the Lord of lords: for His <u>mercy</u> endures forever"*

Vocabulary: <u>mercy</u>

Songs: <u>Stephen: Forgive, Forgive</u>, The Wonder Kids, *20 Bible Heroes Vol. 5*

Snack: <u>Mercy</u> Trains: various foods, make little trains for snack. Bananas, Teddy Grahams, Mini Pop Tarts, mini Ritz Crackers, squeeze cheese. See photo.

Story: Show a Little <u>Mercy</u>, It was Shane's birthday! Shane loves trains, and his birthday gift was a Thomas the Train and track set. Shane got to play with his trains while his cousins were there. The party was great! There was cake, ice cream and presents. The hardest thing about a birthday party is having to share those brand new toys. Shane knew he had to share his new train. His cousin, Jadon loves trains, too. Shane shared his train with Jadon. The boys played trains for a long time. When Jadon looked across the room, he noticed his mom and dad were getting ready to leave. Jadon dropped the new train and ran to the door to his mom and dad. When the train was dropped, it broke into two pieces. Shane was so sad that his new train was broken. Jadon was so sad that he had broken the new train. Both boys began to cry. All the moms and dads were trying to make the boys feel better. Shane knew Jadon didn't mean to break his train. All of a sudden, Shane stood up and walked over to Jadon. Shane gave him a great big hug full of love. "I forgive you, Jadon." Shane showed <u>mercy</u> to Jadon, full of forgiveness and love. That's how God is with us. His love is 'great big' and 'endless'. He gives it freely every minute of every day. Even when we aren't in a good place, God shows us <u>mercy</u>.

Fine Motor: Love and <u>Mercy</u>: trace each child's hands and cut out. Make a large heart and cut out. Wrinkle the hands to look as though the hands are holding the heart. This shows how freely God gives His love and <u>mercy</u>.

Large Motor: <u>Mercy</u> Soccer: use a beach ball to play soccer indoors or outdoors. Use <u>mercy</u> to keep the ball calm and on the ground. Use <u>mercy</u> to be sure the ball is easily controlled by all kids who are playing! <u>Mercy</u> is extra love in <u>Mercy</u> Soccer!

Activity: Draw pictures and write letters to children in the hospital. This is an act of <u>mercy</u> to those who are suffering.

Close in Prayer: Dear Father, Thank You for showing us extra <u>mercy</u> in all ways. You are a loving God. Thank You for sending your only Son, Jesus to the Earth for us. We love You, your Son, Jesus, and your Holy Spirit. Amen

Guidance for Parents: # Mercy

Scripture: Psalm 136:3, *"give thanks to the Lord of lords: for His <u>mercy</u> endures forever"*

Teachable Moment: <u>Mercy</u> is love. <u>Mercy</u> is grace. <u>Mercy</u> is forgiveness. <u>Mercy</u> is acceptance. Mercy is withholding judgement. How does a parent decide if an action requires <u>mercy</u> or consequences?

1. Is the child in danger?

2. How serious is the action?

3. How will society view the action?

4. Is this action reoccurring too often?

5. Is this action a teachable moment that is age appropriate for your child?

6. Does this action have a logical consequence?

7. Does this action have a definite consequence as an adult?

Do not rewrite rules for your child. Meaning: if a rule exists in society, DO NOT make exceptions for your child. Your child must be expected to follow the authority and the rules in place, in any given situation.

Teach: We are free to make choices. We are not free of consequences for those choices. Make good choices!

Ephesians 3:14-19, *Guide me, Lord, as I disciple my children and prepare them for the battles they face everywhere, including their own hearts.*

Songs used today: <u>Stephen: Forgive, Forgive</u>, The Wonder Kids, *20 Bible Heroes Vol. 5*

Vocabulary Builder: <u>mercy</u>

Bible Usage: The word <u>Mercy</u> is used in the Bible 341 times.

Psalm 136:3
...give thanks to the
Lord, for His
mercy endures forever.

Use with <u>Love and Mercy</u> in Lesson 29 – <u>Mercy</u>

Use with <u>Mercy Trains</u> in Lesson 29 – <u>Mercy</u>

Lesson 30

Opening Prayer: Dear Father God, Thank You for inviting us into your <u>kingdom</u>! We want to live with You and sit beside your wonderful Son, Jesus! Amen

Scripture: Romans 14:17, *For the <u>kingdom</u> of God is (not a matter of eating and drinking but) of righteousness and peace and joy in the Holy Spirit*

Vocabulary: <u>kingdom</u>

Songs: <u>Let Your Light Shine</u>, Hillsong Kids, *Ultimate Collection, Live*

<u>My God is so Big, Various Artists</u>, Songs Kids Love to Sing, *25 Bible Action Stories*

<u>His Banner Over Me is Love</u>, The Wonder Kids, *30 Bible Songs and 30 Bible Stories*

Snack: Cracker Castles: use different shaped crackers to create a castle. Give the kids peanut butter to dip the crackers in for 'glue.'

Story: <u>Castle of Gold</u>, *(This is an interactive story to be acted by all kids at once. Paint a Castle Gold!)* God has prepared a beautiful home for each of us. Some people think it will be like a beautiful castle! Jesus lives with His Father in the castle. God invites each one of us to come live with Him in His <u>Kingdom</u>. Here is the good news! God wants His <u>kingdom</u> to be on Earth as it is in Heaven! We can choose to live with Him in his beautiful world right here on Earth. Here's how: every day when we wake up, we should say hello to God. *(Have puppets walk to the castle and knock on the door.)* God will answer the door. Begin talking to God about what you are thankful for. *(Each child should speak for their puppet to tell God what they are thankful for.)* Talk to Him all day long. He is the King! God asks His Son, Jesus to come to the door with Him. Jesus is the Prince of Peace. Jesus asks the Holy Spirit to come to the door with Him. The Holy Spirit is invisible and lives inside of us! The Three in One invites all of us into the castle. We all like it there! It is beautiful, peaceful and the happiest place we have ever been. We all dance and sing! We talk to Jesus. We worship God. We listen to the Holy Spirit. We want to stay all day and all night. All too soon we know we have to go back to our houses. We have to go back with our mommies and daddies. But we know now, that God's Kingdom lives inside of us. We bring God's kingdom down to Earth with us. We live God's way every day. We are joyful in His presence and we listen to His word. We treat others kindly and with love. We are so happy to be a part of God's kingdom!

Fine Motor: God's Kingdom: make a castle out of a brown paper bag. Use the bag to place objects and people that belong to God's Kingdom. (Lesson: The whole world belongs to God. The whole universe belongs to God. God created the world and everything in it. People who choose to follow God and follow His rules are part of God's kingdom.)

Large Motor: God's Kingdom : Make a castle out of cardboard and label it God's Kingdom. Play inside. Use a toy tunnel to lead to the door for extra movement.

Activity: Create a Kingdom: Give each child a piece of sandpaper and pieces of yarn cut different lengths. Have the kids use the string to make the shape of a castle or kingdom on the sandpaper. (squares and triangles)

Close in Prayer: The Lord's Prayer, Matthew 6:9-13

Guidance for Parents: # Kingdom

Scripture: Romans 14:17, *For the <u>kingdom</u> of God is (not a matter of eating and drinking but) of righteousness and peace and joy in the Holy Spirit*

Teachable Moment:

Creation Story: The whole world was created by God. The whole universe was created by God. God created the world and everything in it. Every knee shall bow... Scripture for <u>kingdom</u>...Philippians 2:10-11, That at the name of Jesus every knee should bow, in Heaven, on Earth, and under the Earth... <u>Kingdom</u> Model: Enjoy making a craft project at home out of packing material painted gold for a model of a <u>kingdom</u>, or use cardboard boxes for a life sized <u>kingdom</u>. The Lord's Prayer, Matthew 6:9-13: Continue teaching your child The Lord's Prayer from memory.

Songs used today: <u>Let Your Light Shine</u>, Hillsong Kids, *Ultimate Collection, Live*

<u>My God is so Big, Various Artists</u>, Songs Kids Love to Sing, *25 Bible Action Stories*

<u>His Banner Over Me is Love</u>, The Wonder Kids, *30 Bible Songs and 30 Bible Stories*

Vocabulary Builder: <u>kingdom</u>

Bible Usage: The word <u>kingdom</u> is used in the Bible 384 times.

Romans 14:17
For the kingdom of God
is...of righteousness
and peace and joy
in the Holy Spirit

Use with Cracker Castles in Lesson 30 - <u>Kingdom</u>

Castle

154

About the Author

"Kim Lyon is loving and caring. She loves to hear of God's truth, power, and Word. She cares for everyone she knows and loves. She is beautiful in God's eyes. She's taught kids for more than thirty years and never met a kid she didn't try to help."

—Rich Lyon, age 14

Kim Lyon has dedicated her life to the education of young children. She has a master's of science degree in early childhood and a bachelor's of science degree in elementary education and English. Kim has taught preschool, kindergarten, first, second, and third grades over thirty-two years of teaching. She is currently opening a day school and caring for infants, toddlers, and young children. She considers this her "continuing education."